# Empowered
## for the Call

## Understanding the
## Dynamics of the Anointing

### by

### Dr. Tim Bagwell

McDougal Publishing is a ministry of The Mc-
Dougal Foundation, Inc., a Maryland nonprofit
corporation dedicated to spreading the Gospel of the
Lord Jesus Christ to as many people as possible in
the shortest time possible.

Published by:

**McDougal Publishing**
P.O. Box 3595
Hagerstown, MD   21742-3595

www.mcdougal.org

ISBN 1-884369-73-1
(Formerly ISBN 0-9654268-0-7)

Printed in United States of America
For worldwide distribution

# DEDICATION

I must give honor to whom honor is due:

To *the memory of my father:*

## HOWELL R. BAGWELL
## (1905-1996)

A pioneer of the Pentecostal movement, he taught me both the importance of the anointing of the Holy Spirit and how to flow in it. I am now reaping the benefits of that heritage. I am what I am today because of the deposit he made in my life.

To *my wife:*

## GAYLA JEAN BAGWELL

My wife has walked every step of this ministry journey with me. She has taught me that the anointing is not just for the times when I stand behind the pulpit, but that being anointed is a twenty-four-hour-a-day lifestyle.

Gayla, thank you for all the sacrifices you have made to allow the call of God to be fulfilled in my life.

# CONTENTS

# FOREWORD BY
# DR. ORAL ROBERTS

I love the title of this new book, *"Empowered for the Call,"* by my close friend in the Lord, Tim Bagwell, for he literally exemplifies the empowerment of the call of God on a believer's life. Tim, as an end-time prophet, pastor, and teacher, attempts nothing without first being anointed to do that job.

I have discovered that the anointing is that divine energy which separates us from ourselves and fills us with the glory of God, so that when we speak, it is like God speaking, and when we act, it is like God acting. With the anointing, any believer, especially a preacher of the Gospel, can bring God's deliverance to the lost and suffering, just as Jesus did when He was on the Earth.

*"Empowered for the Call"* comes out of the anointing of Tim Bagwell, and it plumbs the depth and breadth of God's anointing power in a way that I believe will inform, strengthen, and encourage those blessed enough to obtain a copy. It is a valuable addition to every Christian's library.

# INTRODUCTION

When God directed me to preach the series of messages on which this book is based, my own personal ministry was flourishing. I was operating in far more power than ever before and seeing God manifest Himself in healing, deliverance, breakthroughs, and blessing. Yet He told me, "When you preach this, your church will be changed and will move into a new level of effectiveness in the Kingdom." I realized that just as God was moving me personally into a new level of anointing and effectiveness, He wanted to do the same for my congregation. After all, God wants His entire Body, not just pastors and leaders, to be raised up. His Word declares it:

> *Moses my servant is dead; now therefore arise, go over this Jordan, THOU, AND ALL THIS PEOPLE, unto the land which I do give to them.*
> Joshua 1:2

I knew that not everyone would be willing to make this move. There will always be those who want the benefits of a promise without making the sacrifice required to obtain those benefits. But there will also always be a remnant of people who love God enough to make any sacrifice to bring His perfect will to pass.

God told me, "If you will obey Me and preach this message, I will change lives and cause men and women to experience a breakthrough in their spirits. I will impact the lives of those who hear you, and they will become rooted, grounded and established." God always means what He says, and I have learned to listen when He speaks.

I prepared my congregation for this move of God by leading them on a six-month journey in His Word. I took authority over the evil powers assigned to retard spiritual development and declared the will of God—that His people would have ears to hear, minds to perceive, and hearts to receive His message.

The series I preached on the anointing proved so effective at Word of Life Christian Center that I began to share it with other churches, and they, too, saw phenomenal results. As devoted saints recognized that God's hand was moving in a special way and prepared their hearts to receive it, He placed a new anointing upon them. That remnant then became truly empowered of God, rooted, grounded and established, as He had promised. This message is now being put into book form so that more of God's people can benefit from the truths it contains.

It is time for the people of God to step forth in all

that the empowerment of the Anointed One represents. It is time for the release of a new mantle of the anointing upon us, time for the entire Church of the Lord Jesus Christ to begin walking, speaking and operating in a demonstration of the empowerment of Almighty God. It is time for us to step forth fearlessly, knowing that we are totally empowered to fulfill the call God has placed upon us in this hour.

May the revelations contained in this work edify the entire Church of the Lord Jesus Christ and be instrumental in raising up the leadership we so desperately need in this critical hour. May it raise you, the readers, to the higher level of the anointing power that God desires for your life and ministry. May you truly be *Empowered for the Call.*

*Tim Bagwell*
*Denver, Colorado*

*And the spirit of the LORD will come upon thee, and thou shalt prophesy with them, and shalt be turned into ANOTHER MAN.*

1 Samuel 10:6

# PART I:

# UNDERSTANDING THE ANOINTING

# THE EMPOWERMENT WHICH ACCOMPANIES YOUR CALL

*For the GIFTS and CALLING of God are without repentance.*                    Romans 11:29

It is impossible to have a call of God without also having the empowerment to carry out that call. It cannot happen. When God calls us, He empowers us to fulfill His call. If you claim that you are called to do some specific task for God, and you don't have His power on your life to perform that task, you are deceived. It simply cannot happen. If you have no empowerment, either you are not truly called, or you have received no revelation of what the Holy Ghost has done in you. The power is there. You must discover it and begin to use it. He who has called you is faithful to empower you for the task.

Jesus was the Anointed One, and He had the greatest outpouring of supernatural manifestation ever recorded as flowing through any man in the history of the world. Yet even He worked no miracles until the empowerment to do those miracles came upon Him.

Luke, the writer of the Acts of the Apostles recorded:

> *How God anointed Jesus of Nazareth with the Holy Ghost and with power: who went about doing good, and healing all that were oppressed of the devil; for God was with him.*     Acts 10:38

He was first anointed, and then He *"went about doing good and healing."*

### EVEN WITNESSING REQUIRES EMPOWERMENT

The empowerment spoken of in Acts 1:8 was for the purpose of making the early believers witnesses. To truly be a witness means not only to testify about the Gospel of Jesus Christ, the Word of God; it means to be empowered by the gift of the Holy Spirit, through the faith of Jesus Christ, to manifest evidence of His life and anointing. Being a witness is more than words coming from your mouth. It involves manifestations, proof of what you are witnessing with your mouth.

Many people talk a lot, but the Bible does not say you are to be a living epistle "heard of all men." It says you are to be a living *"epistle ... known and read of all men"* (2 Corinthians 3:2). If you are to be His witness, there must be, at some point, a demonstration of God's power coming forth from your life to back up what you are saying. A proclamation demands a demonstration.

When the anointing of God comes upon your life, the empowerment it represents will change you. Physical weariness lifts as the power of the Holy Spirit takes your natural and makes it supernatural. As a result, you walk and talk, think and act differently. You are no longer afraid of demons, disease or depression. You have supernatural boldness and can look beyond the rebukes and the rejection of men. You have what it takes to lift burdens and destroy yokes.

### CARRYING TWINS

The anointing in you is very much like human conception, and when you become impregnated with an anointing, you find yourself carrying twins. Baby "Call" and Baby "Gifting" are both growing inside of you.

As these two babies grow, Baby "Call" begins kicking and moving, stirring in your innermost being. He is letting you know that he is getting bigger every day and that there is coming a time appointed by the Father for him to be brought forth. When that days comes, Baby "Call" will no longer be just the *"substance of things hoped for."* He will become a living, breathing reality manifested in your life. You will begin to feel an urgency to pray for sick people, to preach the Gospel to those who have not yet heard it, and to lay hands on people who are oppressed and see them delivered.

But how will you accomplish all this? Just when you begin to wonder if you will really ever be able to do anything of lasting value, suddenly Baby "Gifting" begins kicking too. He is reminding you that you *"can do all things through Christ who strengthens [you],"* that God distributes the gifts *"severally as He will,"* and that *"greater is He that is in [you] than he that is in the world."*

Suddenly the realization will strike you: you don't just have a call in you, you also have the power in you to fulfill that call and to accomplish the purpose of God for your life. The call and the empowerment always go together, and when God gives one, He gives the other — without fail.

When the time has come for you to step out into your God-given destiny, when the Holy Ghost says, "Separate Me this vessel for the particular mission for which he was born and for which I saved and delivered him," you will not be lacking power. That's God's promise. Whether your call is to teach a class, to go to the mission field, or to lay hands on the sick, you can count on the fact that an impartation of Holy Ghost power will come into your life specifically for that task. You will never have to go forth to do God's work without the power to do it.

If you love the Lord and have given Him your heart, you have a God vocation. The word "call" used in the New Testament comes from the Greek word *kaleo* which relates to "vocation" and "destination." Your vocation may or may not be the way you earn your living. Your particular God vocation may be in intercession, music, teaching children, street witnessing, exhorting new believers, working with young people, helping the elderly, or serving in some other capacity in the House of God. But whatever the call, you have the special anointing that coincides with it.

## THE REVELATION MAY PRECEDE THE GIFTING

The Word of God declares: *"For the gifts and calling of God are without repentance."* It does not say "the gifts ... are without repentance" or "the call ... is without repentance." The two go together: *"the gifts and calling of God are without repentance."* God never calls anyone that He does not empower for that call and God does not empower anyone without purpose. The gifts and the call work together, the one making possible the completion of the other.

The revelation of the call may indeed come first. It may precede the empowerment. But be assured that when the time comes to go forth and do the work, God will not send you out without the proper tools to accomplish your task.

David received the revelation that he was to be king of Israel long before the empowerment became obvious. But when it came time for him to take his rightful place as king, the empowerment was there. God would never call someone to a position of ministry and send them forth before He first had empowered them to perform that ministry. He just would not do that.

When you are called of God, you have a spiritual vocation and a spiritual destination. Therefore, God must get you to your destination and empower you to fulfill your vocation. He must empower you to see burdens removed and yokes destroyed. If you tried to arrive at your spiritual destination and operate in your spiritual vocation without an anointing from God, your efforts would surely be futile. If any man even imagines that he can fulfill his divine destiny, his call of service to God, without supernatural intervention, he is sadly mistaken. And there is no reason for us to even try. God is ready and willing to empower us for every task.

You may have seen people in some aspect of ministry who seemed to lack gifts to perform their chosen work. If so, it may well be that they were not called to that work. Maybe it was their own choice, not God's. If you know someone who went to a foreign country to work as a missionary and is ready to go home after only a few weeks there, you can probably be sure that they were not called of God to that place. Those who are called have the supernatural strength to persevere.

It's dangerous to call yourself to any work, let alone to some foreign lands. You cannot just get up one day and decide to travel halfway around the world and expect to have a new missionary anointing. That's not how it works. It takes a special empowerment to be a missionary. God does the calling, and He must do the anointing. If you are not truly called, you will not be empowered, and if you are not empowered, you will be broken in the process of trying to do something you cannot possibly do.

When God calls you, when He says, "This is the task I have put before you," then He becomes responsible for the outcome and must empower you to successfully fulfill that call. If you have called yourself, however, your failure is not God's fault.

When you are truly called and truly sent, you need not fear the task. You are empowered for that purpose and you have no reason to fear the future in any way.

## THE DANGER OF BEING SELF-CALLED

If you are not seeing any manifestation of the giftings and empowerment of God in the calling in which you are operating, ask yourself where that call came from. You may have gone to Bible school, and that is a good thing. But the fact that you sat through Bible school doesn't mean you are called to be a preacher, any more than sitting in a garage means you were called to be a car. Keeping company with a group of people who operate in the prophetic realm will not necessarily make you a prophet. Attending healing seminars will not necessarily make you the next Oral Roberts.

While it is true that there can be spiritual impartation into your life from anointed men and women of God, and there is spiritual edification for all those who sit under the tutelage of great men and women of faith, God is the One Who anoints. It is God who gifts those whom He calls and provides them the power to fulfill His desires.

He does this before He sends you forth. He never fails in this respect. He wants you to be *Empowered For the Call*.

# DEFINING THE ANOINTING

*The spirit of the LORD God is upon me; because THE LORD HATH ANOINTED ME to preach good tidings unto the meek; he hath sent me to bind up the brokenhearted, to proclaim liberty to the captives, and the opening of the prison to them that are bound; To proclaim the acceptable year of the LORD, and the day of vengeance of our God; to comfort all that mourn;* Isaiah 61:1-2

Since the anointing is so important, making all the difference between success and failure in our personal lives, as well as in our ministries, it is wise for us to understand it well. Several important questions must be answered:

## WHAT IS THE ANOINTING?

The anointing is an empowerment from God which allows a natural man — body, soul and spirit

— to act supernaturally. The word "anointing" comes from the Greek word *chrio,* which means "to smear or rub with oil." In Old Testament times a literal oil was used to anoint those who would serve God in any capacity. That oil, however, was symbolic of the Holy Spirit, for it is the Spirit who empowers us to act.

There are several derivatives of this root word *chrio* that are also used in the Bible to speak of the anointing. The *enchrio* or "rubbing in" refers to the anointing in us which is for our own personal edification, and the *epichrio* or "rubbing on" refers to the anointing upon us to minister to others. Both are equally important to believers, as we shall see.

This passage from Isaiah foretold the anointing which would be upon Jesus. Jesus, from His first recorded sermon (preached from this very text), revealed the fulfillment of Isaiah's promise. He was the Anointed One; and His message, the Gospel of the Anointing, is the same message we should be proclaiming today, for it is the message that sets men and women free.

In biblical days the act of anointing someone with oil was recognized as a means of transferring divine power and authority to those chosen to do God's work. It also represented a bestowal of God's favor and an impartation of His holiness and virtue. These dynamics of the anointing of God — power, authority, favor, virtue and holiness — are all part of the empowerment that God desires to give each of His children to enable us to live victorious personal lives and to carry out His work in the Earth.

## WHAT IS THE PURPOSE OF THE ANOINTING?

*And it shall come to pass in that day, that his burden shall be taken away from off thy shoulder, and his yoke from off thy neck, and the yoke shall be destroyed because of the anointing.*

Isaiah 10:27

The purpose of the anointing is made so absolutely clear in the Scriptures that it might be considered "the law of the anointing." It is the sure yardstick by which all ministry can be measured. When the anointing is present, burdens will be removed and yokes will be destroyed. It's just that cut and dried. Since the anointing is a power, a dynamic, we can recognize it by what it accomplishes.

The purpose of the anointing of God in your personal life is to lift your burdens and destroy your yokes, and the purpose of God's power upon you in ministerial gifts is to lift the burdens of others and to destroy their yokes. You can do this because, when you are anointed, you bear God's power, His authority, His favor, His virtue and His holiness. The result is that you do the works of Christ, the Anointed One.

If you are a preacher and your preaching is anointed, it will lift burdens and destroy yokes. If you are a singer and your singing is anointed, it will lift burdens and destroy yokes. The same holds true for teaching, personal ministry or whatever else you put your hand to. Anything that is anointed will bear fruit, because the anointing always accomplishes something for God. Anything done in the power, authority, favor, holiness and virtue of God will result in burdens being lifted and yokes being destroyed. That is the law of the anointing.

The Hebrew word used for anointing in this text from Isaiah is unique. It is only used in this reference and in the Twenty-third Psalm. It is *shemen*, which translates as "richness or fatness." When we are truly empowered by God, we are enriched and enlarged. Our destiny in Him is far greater than our destiny without Him. He enriches us beyond words and enlarges us beyond expectation. He loves us, cares about us and is *"touched with the feelings of our infirmities."* He knows that we cannot fulfill His call upon our lives if we are burdened down and shackled.

Israel was an anointed nation, yet she found herself, at times, under the yoke of foreign enemies. In this reference, it was the Assyrian Empire which was oppressing God's people, but God said that this burden would be lifted and the yoke would be destroyed because of the anointing — the power, authority, favor, holiness, and virtue of God. His people would be free because of the greatness and richness of the God who had anointed them.

If we expect to understand why God is anointing us and what He wants to accomplish through that anointing, we must look beyond the hot flashes, the cold chills and the other unusual feelings or sensations we have when we sense His anointing upon us. The anointing, the empowerment of God, has been placed in our lives because each of us has an eternal destiny, and that destiny is to live a life of signs, wonders and miracles. We are destined to see the hand of God at work in a burden-lifting, yoke-destroying visitation on our own lives and the lives of those living around us. This God-ordained prophetic promise for your life is more important to God than anything else about you. God wants to lift your burden and break your yoke because of the calling that is upon your life and because of the sacred destiny He has pronounced over you.

When God first showed me this truth, I saw the yoke the enemy was trying to put around the neck of God's people and I saw that neck expanding until the yoke simply would not fit. Your destiny is greater than the yoke the enemy tries to put on you. It is greater than anything that tries to hinder you..

## WHAT IS THE SOURCE OF THE ANOINTING?

*For all the promises of God in him are yea, and in him Amen, unto the glory of God by us. Now he*

*which stablisheth us with you in Christ, and hath
anointed us, is God; Who hath also sealed us, and
given the earnest of the Spirit in our hearts.*

2 Corinthians 1:20-22

Although oil was used symbolically in Bible days,
and although it was applied by a man — usually a
prophet or other servant of the Lord — it was, nev-
ertheless, widely-recognized by the Israelites that the
true anointing, the resultant empowerment, came
directly from God and from Him alone. We cannot
anoint ourselves. There is nothing in our mind, flesh
or emotions that can empower us to do the work of
God. Therefore, the anointing is not something that
can be either worked up or thought up. It cannot
come from the intellect or the emotions. Although
we may feel the anointing when it comes upon us,
the anointing itself is totally unrelated to feeling. It
is God's empowerment upon our lives — whether
we feel it or not.

Some churches put a premium on intellectualism
or education, but it makes no difference how bril-
liant a person may be, how high his IQ, or how many
degrees hang on his office wall. The anointing is not
to be found in any of these. Knowledge and education are one thing, and the anointing is something
entirely different. A person cannot become anointed
by attending the right school or even the right semi-
nary. The anointing comes only from God.

## Defining the Anointing

The anointing is totally unrelated to position in the community, financial success, employment status or possessions. It is not related in any way to our appearance. Even faithful church attendance, while an important factor in our walk with the Lord, cannot assure us of the anointing. He who anoints us is God, and there is no other way to get the anointing.

Often people tend to confuse the anointing with other natural characteristics or virtues, but it takes more than a charismatic personality or exceptional talent to be anointed by God. While God can anoint our personalities and natural talents and make them effective for Him, our personalities and talents alone will not make us anointed.

Family relationships cannot make us anointed. Being the child of an anointed man or woman does not automatically make a person anointed. No matter how anointed your mother may be, no matter how long she spends on her knees interceding for you, it is still God who must do the anointing. Without Him, we are nothing.

Each of us must realize that although intelligence is good, education is good, being talented is good, being well-organized is good, being blessed financially is good, none of these is the source of divine power and authority. None of these can bestow on us the favor of our heavenly Father or bring us an impartation of His virtue and holiness.

Concerning the church, we must remember that while it is good to maintain proper order, work to increase membership, attempt to utilize modern technology and recruit talented church leaders, none of these will prove to be the source of the anointing that we so desperately need today. In the closing days of the twentieth century, it is still necessary to keep reminding men and women of faith that it is not the external trappings of the church that give us power with God and that we must continually look to the Source for our anointing.

Even Jesus had to depend on the Father for His anointing. There is no record of His having worked any miracles before He was thirty. The first recorded miracle in His ministry took place after He came up out of the waters of baptism in the Jordan River and, from that moment, Jesus could honestly say, *"The Spirit of the Lord is upon Me."* It was shortly after this that miraculous things began to be manifested in His life and ministry.

Understanding what the anointing is, what it does and where it comes from is an important first step in being *Empowered for the Call.*

# THREE LEVELS OF ANOINTING

There are three levels or phases of an anointing through which we must pass in order to arrive at the place of power and authority God has destined for us. They are the anointing of revelation, the anointing of preparation, and the anointing of destination.

## THE ANOINTING OF REVELATION

*THE SPIRIT ITSELF BEARETH WITNESS WITH OUR SPIRIT, that we are the children of God: And if children, then heirs; heirs of God, and joint-heirs with Christ; if so be that we suffer with him, that we may be also glorified together.*

Romans 8:16-17

You are not really alive until you have received the revelation of who you are in God and of His eternal plan for your life. Receiving such a revelation

can be likened to a seed being conceived in a womb.
The Spirit, as Paul tells us, *"beareth witness with our
spirit that we are the children of God."* That means there
is a coming together of our spirit and God's Spirit
that might be considered a parallel of the natural
process of conception. Unless the egg and the sperm
are joined, no life can be formed in the womb, and
unless God's Spirit and ours is united, there can be
no spiritual life in us and no God-ordained purpose
for our existence.

Your spirit is the eternal dynamic within you, and
as God begins to speak to you about your call, about
your ministry, about the things He wants you to do
with your life, your spirit is crying out to conceive
the revelation. The Bible tells us that men are
groaning and travailing within their spirits for *"the
manifestation of the sons of God"*:

> *For the earnest expectation of the creature waiteth
> for the manifestation of the sons of God.*
> *For we know that the whole creation groaneth and
> travaileth in pain together until now. And not
> only they, but ourselves also, which have the
> firstfruits of the Spirit, even we ourselves groan
> within ourselves, waiting for the adoption, to wit,
> the redemption of our body.*
>
> Romans 8:19, 22-23

Like the egg within the natural womb, our spirit
is crying out, "I am here. My purpose is to be united

with the Spirit of God. Only then can I be fruitful." When our spirits unite with God's Spirit and we come into agreement with Him, life is created. When God has spoken a word into your life — whether through a vision, a dream, a prophetic word or a divine revelation, you will sense His empowering presence begin to touch your life.

When you feel God's presence and receive His word, His revelation, or His vision, something rises up inside of you, and your spirit cries out, "Let new life be conceived." The anointing will begin to work on you right at that moment, lifting the burdens and destroying the yokes, abolishing the spirit of fear, and putting faith into operation.

Just as a natural mother's entire being responds and changes after conception, you will feel different after a seed of revelation has been conceived in you. Hopelessness will lift, confusion will lift, childishness will lift and spiritual desperation will be removed because you have heard from God and have begun digesting what He has told you. You will feel more alive than you have ever felt before.

While our spirits are crying out to conceive, however, our carnal mind, our flesh, wants to abort the seed of revelation. Flesh doesn't want to pay the price that must be paid for conception. It would rather see this seed of revelation aborted, so that it can go on living in the present comfort zone.

When God reveals to you His will for your life —
to see the sick recover or to stand in a foreign nation
and preach the Gospel to other tribes, races and cul-
tures — your natural mind will tell you it can never
happen. It will try to convince you that you will always be stuck in a little cubical void of faith.
Everything about your natural being will want to
kill that dream, that vision, that plan of God.

Your flesh is inspired by the master abortionist,
Satan himself. The devil is intent on aborting your
anointing of revelation. When he moves quickly to
try to pull you into discouragement and disbelief,
it's not just because he happened to draw your name
out of a hat. It's because he knows more about your
destiny and the ultimate life being conceived by your
revelation than you know yourself.

While your natural man is still trying to figure
out whether you have really heard from God, and
while your spirit is trying to convince you that you
have, the enemy is also listening. He knows God's
word is true, so he doesn't hesitate for a moment.
He launches his attack — swiftly and fiercely.

One of the first weapons Satan will use against
you is a feeling of hopelessness. He wants to bog
you down in past defeats or current circumstances.
You must realize that when revelation comes it has
nothing to do with circumstances. It has nothing to
do with your track record. You must allow the seed
of that revelation God gave you to be conceived in

your spiritual being, nothing more, and God will do the rest.

### THE ANOINTING OF PREPARATION

*Now I say, That the heir, as long as he is a child, differeth nothing from a servant, though he be lord of all; But is under tutors and governors until the time appointed of the father.* Galatians 4:1-2

The next level or phase in the anointing is the anointing of preparation. God cannot bring you to your destination unless He first makes you ready.

When David had the anointing oil poured over him in approximately 1063 B.C., that was his anointing of revelation. From 1063 B.C. to 1048 B.C., he experienced a preparation anointing, and it proved to be a very difficult time for him. It often seemed as if he were walking through the very fires of Hell. During this time, God had to reaffirm to David that he was indeed the chosen of the Lord. David had to learn not to try to do things in his own way, but to totally trust the Lord in every situation.

The hard times David experienced in preparation for greatness were typical of what each of us may go through. Once the revelation is conceived, and we know that we are the sons of God and the sons of destiny, God may deal rather harshly with us. Many shrink from this chastening, but it is a necessary part of our training. Unless we can endure the chastening of the Lord, we are not legitimate sons:

*And ye have forgotten the exhortation which speaketh unto you as unto children, My son, despise not thou the chastening of the Lord, nor faint when thou art rebuked of him: For whom the Lord loveth he chasteneth, and scourgeth every son whom he receiveth. If ye endure chastening, God dealeth with you as with sons; for what son is he whom the father chasteneth not? But if ye be without chastisement, whereof all are partakers, then are ye bastards, and not sons.* Hebrews 12:5-8

Sometimes we moan and groan over the tests and trials and battles we must face, but that is all part of our badge of authentication. Far too many people expect to rise to the fullness of their destiny without first allowing time for preparation, for the application of the anointing to the weaknesses of our flesh, emotions and attitudes. That anointing is present to lift our burdens and break the yokes of carnal-mindedness. If we fail to allow the Spirit of God to build the *enchrio* within us, we might end up like King Saul, rejected of God and divested of all divine authority.

God said: *"the heir, as long as he is a child, differeth nothing from a servant, though he be lord of all."* God cannot use you if you do not allow Him to prepare you first. An immature person with a godly destination is no different from a person with an ungodly destination. When you get a real revelation of what God wants to do with your life, immaturity must begin to lift from you. You must get serious with God. As long as you remain immature, you will never possess your prophetic heritage, and your destiny will be nothing more than a dream. It is only when the Lord sees maturity in your life — marked by diligence, holiness and a desire to please Him — that He can entrust to you the blessings of your inheritance.

Joseph is another good example. He had to endure an extensive anointing of preparation before he could step into his destination. He had to pass through the pit and the prison before his revelation, received as a teenager, became reality. He might have been forgiven for thinking that God had forgotten him at times; but when we think that God has forgotten about us, the truth is that He is just making us ready for greater things.

When you get frustrated and discouraged because you don't see the quick fulfillment of some of the things you know God has spoken to you, imagine how David and Joseph must have felt. God wanted them to experience a thorough anointing of preparation because the destination He had planned for them was great, and His Word declares:

## Empowered For the Call

*For unto whomsoever much is given, of him shall be much required.*                    Luke 12:48

You will never step into your destination without first experiencing an anointing of preparation. When you, on the other hand, allow God the time He requires to prepare you, you will be able to accomplish more for Him in one year than you could have done in a lifetime without that preparation.

### THE ANOINTING OF DESTINATION

Every person reading this book, regardless of age, has a destination in God. You can be assured that God will anoint you for a specific day and hour that He has prepared for you — if you are willing to pay whatever price comes with that call.

For those who have already accomplished great things for God, there are greater days ahead. David's ministry did not end when he was anointed king over Israel; that was just the beginning. Joseph's ministry did not end when he was made second in command in Egypt; it was just beginning. If you have been blessed and have been able to accomplish something for God, know that you have not yet stepped into the fullness of the benefits of your call, your true anointing of destination. There are greater things ahead for each of us.

## Three Levels of Anointing

When we step into an anointing of destination, our personal lives are often violated because we are no longer free to do what we want to do. When we know that someone has a need and that they are counting on us to minister to them, and that someone is looking to us for mentoring or discipling, it changes our lives dramatically.

There is a price to pay to walk in an anointing of destination, and that price is responsibility. When rivers of living water dwell in your innermost being, you have a responsibility to pour them out.

There is a price to pay, and that price is unseating flesh from his position as lord of your life and enthroning the Lord Jesus in his stead. Your anointing and obedience to the calling that brought that anointing to your life become more important to you than anything else.

When you step into your anointing of destination, you will know it. Something supernatural will begin happening at a whole new level. A very different kind of power will come over your ministry and, from that point on, it will blossom and flourish.

You can begin right now, even before the manifestation of that anointing, to see yourself as an anointed man or woman of God. If you feel you are destined to pastor or to evangelize or to perform some other ministry and the time has not yet come, tell the person you see in your mirror, "I am anointed. God has not forgotten me. He is just making me ready. My time is coming. He is fitting me for the Master's service, and I am willing to pay that price. Very soon now He will launch me into my anointing of destination, and I will be *Empowered for the Call*."

# THE ANOINTING IN YOU FOR YOUR OWN EDIFICATION

*I counsel thee to buy of me gold tried in the fire,*
*that thou mayest be rich; and white raiment, that*
*thou mayest be clothed, and that the shame of thy*
*nakedness do not appear; and ANOINT THINE*
*EYES WITH EYESALVE, that thou mayest see.*

Revelation 3:18

There is a deposit of the Holy Spirit in you that is for the express purpose of enriching your personal life, and there is a deposit of the power of God upon your life that enables you to minister to others. When you begin to understand the difference between the workings of these two anointings, you will be able to go *"from glory to glory."* It is the *enchrio*, the anointing in you for you, that is the focus of this chapter.

This passage, which speaks of anointing the *"eyes with eyesalve,"* does not refer to natural eyes, but to spiritual eyes. When God's anointing is applied to our lives, our spiritual eyesight is enhanced and our spiritual hearing is sharpened. God said through John:

*He that hath an ear, let him hear what the Spirit saith unto the churches.* Revelation 2:7

It is quite possible to have ears and still not hear. The *enchrio* brings spiritual empowerment to the inner man, causing him to be more keen to the things of God.

Another area affected by the anointing is our thinking. Paul wrote to the Church:

*Let this mind be in you, which was also in Christ Jesus.* Philippians 2:5

Christ, the Anointed One, had an anointed mind, and God is calling upon each of us to seek to be anointed in this same way. God's anointing can dramatically change our thinking, as we are *"transformed by the renewing of [our] minds"*:

*And be not conformed to this world: but be ye transformed by the renewing of your mind, that ye may prove what is that good, and acceptable, and perfect, will of God.* Romans 12:2

# The Anointing in You for Your Own Edification

## THE *ENCHRIO* BRINGS HOLINESS

Most of us would like to walk a little holier before the Lord. We would like to have His character and His nature. Many are coming to the conclusion, however, that this is impossible. "It's too hard to live for God," many say these days, and that's true — unless you are anointed and have submitted the old fleshly man to the empowerment of God. It *is* too hard to live for God — unless you have experienced burdens being removed and yokes being destroyed through God's anointing. If you receive a rubbing in of the anointing, so that the inner man is impacted by the authority, power, favor, holiness and virtue of the Lord God, it is no longer difficult or impossible to live right.

When you are anointed, you will tap into God's holiness. Too many people are trying to be holy in their own strength, and they simply cannot do it in the flesh. That's what grace is all about. It is the ability of God to do for you what you cannot do for yourself. When you begin walking in grace, you will find that you have the ability to live right.

Face it: a life of godly character requires the *enchrio* or "rubbing in" of the anointing of God into your inner man. Too many people struggle with this because they won't let God get close enough to them so He can rub it in. Instead, they want to stay in control of their lives, dictating their own destiny and telling God what's right and what's wrong. Having the anointing of God loosed in your life requires dying to yourself.

When God looked upon Joshua, He said, "Here's Joshua, a man in whom is the Spirit." Why was the Spirit of God so identifiable in Joshua, while it may not have been as readily identifiable in others? A person receives whatever they open themselves to, and Joshua had opened himself to the Spirit of God and allowed his spirit to conceive a revelation inside of him. Consequently, God liked what He saw in Joshua.

When you allow God's Spirit to work on the inside of you, things start changing — attitudes and outlooks, your walk and your talk, and even your appetites. You begin to abhor sin, to hate the things of the flesh, the same things you once loved.

When the twelve spies came back from looking over the Promised Land, ten of them were saying, "There's no way we can take this land. We would be eaten alive by these giants." Two of the twelve men, however, came back with a very different attitude. They said, "What are we waiting for? Let's take the land right now." One of those men was Joshua, whom the Lord had called *"a man in whom is the Spirit."* The other man was Caleb. Of him, the Lord said:

*But my servant Caleb, because he had another spirit with him, and hath followed me fully, him*

*will I bring into the land whereinto he went; and*
*his seed shall possess it.*　　　Numbers 14:24

All twelve of the spies Moses chose were Jews. They were all warriors with similar garments and similar armor. Yet, there was obviously a major difference between two of them, Joshua and Caleb, and the other ten. What caused that difference? The difference between these men had nothing to do with their parentage or their genetic heritage. It had nothing to do with their natural armament or training. The difference was inside, in the spirit man. They were anointed by God.

## THE *ENCHRIO* BRINGS BLESSINGS

When the Lord looked at Joshua and saw a man in whom the Spirit was evident, a man whom He could trust with greater empowerment, He declared a blessing upon him. When the Lord looked at Caleb and saw that he, too, had a different spirit than the other spies, that the Holy Spirit was inside him, He told Caleb that he and his seed would possess the land. It happened because he had an anointing inside him which kept changing him.

Those two men, Joshua and Caleb, were different because they had an anointing that was for their personal edification, an *enchrio*, the anointing in them for them. That same anointing was available to the other spies. The difference was that Joshua and Caleb opened themselves to God's Spirit.

The inward anointing, the *enchrio*, mortifies your flesh, allowing you to maintain an intimate relationship with God. It lifts your burdens and destroys your yokes. It opens your spiritual eyes so that you can see, unstops your spiritual ears so that you can hear and causes your mind to be transformed into the mind of Christ. It causes *"every thought"* to be brought *"into captivity ... to the obedience of Christ"* (2 Corinthians 10:5). Why is this important? So that you can be conformed to the image and likeness of Christ, changed into a man like Adam was before he fell into sin. So that you can have dominion. So that there can be a transference of power and authority, a bestowal of favor and a release of holiness and virtue upon your life.

As the anointing inside of you begins to mortify your flesh, you begin to want God to use you, and if you really want to be used of God, you must let Him shake you. You must let Him break you. You must actually let God kill you and make you over into a totally new creation.

Your *enchrio*, the anointing in you for your personal edification, makes you much like a caterpillar. The caterpillar must first go through a metamorphosis into the cocoon stage. At that stage, it takes the form of something not so pleasant. Caterpillars are destructive, but God knows how to turn caterpillars into butterflies. God knows how to dissolve the body of the caterpillar and recreate it.

If you truly desire to be used of God, there must come a time when you say, "Lord, You're going to have to kill the caterpillar nature in me. I want to be used of You more than anything else, but I know that in order for You to use me, You must see the Spirit of God within me."

When you say, "I want to be used of God," you should consider whether or not you are really willing to be dissolved. Are you willing to go into a secret place, a dark place, where nobody can get to you but God?

The Bible says:

> But ye are a chosen generation, a royal priesthood, an holy nation, a peculiar people; that ye should show forth the praises of him who hath called you out of darkness into his marvellous light:
>
> 1 Peter 2:9

We are *"called ... out of darkness."* And darkness is the place where God dissolves your flesh, the place where He changes you, the place where the destructive caterpillar is slowly turned into a butterfly.

A butterfly is a thing of beauty and uniqueness, and when God brings you out of the dark place and loosens you by the power of the Spirit, He can place His honor on you because you are a new person.

Your anointing, the one that is in you for you, has killed you. It has mortified your flesh, and God has given you new life.

## The *Enchrio* Brings Revelation

It is the *enchrio* that brings about revelation in your life and enables you to go through the preparation so that you can eventually arrive at a destination in God. Paul wrote:

> *Eye hath not seen, nor ear heard, neither have entered into the heart of man, the things which God hath prepared for them that love him. But God hath revealed them unto us by his Spirit: for the Spirit searcheth all things, yea, the deep things of God.* 1 Corinthians 2:9-10

There comes a time when it becomes necessary to shut the door, get on your face before God and say, "Holy Spirit, start opening this thing up to me." When a revelation comes to you through a pastor or prophet, it may reach your spirit in part, but first it must be processed through your intellect so that you can judge whether or not it's from God. But when the Holy Ghost talks to you directly, the words will burn in your spirit and the message of the words will shake you from the crown of your head to the soles of your feet. Your anointing brings revelation, and revelation will change you.

## The Anointing in You for Your Own Edification

### THE *ENCHRIO* BRINGS EDIFICATION

The anointing in you will also bring edification. It will make it possible for you to encourage yourself. When you are betrayed, lied about or buried under the burdens of life, the Bible says the Holy Spirit will intercede for you *"with groanings which cannot be uttered"* (Romans 8:26).

When you are so beat up that you don't even know how to talk to God, the Holy Ghost will take over. Suddenly, even when you are bent over and burdened, your anointing starts stirring inside of you. Suddenly, your hands start going up toward Heaven. Your flesh is saying. "I don't want to pray," but your anointing starts bubbling and churning and stirring down inside of you, and suddenly you are built up and strengthened.

When you allow God to put that different Spirit within you, you will begin to devote yourself to the integrity of God. This will cause every muscle in your spiritual anatomy to be strengthened. Then, when the enemy comes against you, you can look at him and say, "I'm going to lift your burden, Satan. I'm going to destroy your yoke because of the anointing in me."

While both the *enchrio* and *epichrio* are equally valid and important empowerments of God, it is essential that you have the first, or you can never flow properly in the second. The first thing God

49

wants to see established in your spirit is character, the godly character that will enable you to walk in the image and likeness of Christ.

Always remember, charisma without character is dangerous.

## The *Enchrio* Protects You From Falling

I am convinced that most ministers who fall into the entrapment of sin and step out of fellowship with God don't do so because they have lost the power in their ministry. Instead, the *enchrio* (the anointing which dealt with their personal walk, the personal burden-lifting, yoke-destroying power of God that has been deposited inside them for their personal benefit) has not been properly attended to.

You cannot gauge your personal spirituality by the results of your ministry, nor by the signs and wonders you see God manifesting through it. You must gauge your spirituality by the holiness, integrity and virtue in your life. If the anointing is in you, it will continually lift burdens and destroy yokes and cause you to be conformed to Christ's image.

The *enchrio* is that inner anointing which keeps the character in the shape it should be in. It keeps spiritual wholeness about you. When the *enchrio* is kept intact over a long period of time, you will be able to confidently say with David:

## The Anointing in You for Your Own Edification

*I have been young, and now am old; yet have I not seen the righteous forsaken, nor his seed begging bread.*                    Psalms 37:25

The man with the greater *enchrio* will have the greater *epichrio*. The man who has the greater anointing *in* him will walk with a greater anointing *upon* him to work the works of God. If you regularly attend to the deposit God has placed within you, you will not stagnate spiritually. You will not hit a certain level and wonder why you can go no higher. As you attend to your *enchrio*, the anointing in you for your personal edification, you will be changed, *Empowered for the Call.*

# THE ANOINTING UPON YOU WHICH ALLOWS YOU TO MINISTER TO OTHERS

*When he had thus spoken, he spat on the ground, and made clay of the spittle, and HE ANOINTED THE EYES OF THE BLIND MAN with the clay.*

John 9:6

The word Jesus used here for anointing is *epichrio*, the Greek word meaning "to rub on." Just as the word *enchrio* was used as a reference for a spiritual "rubbing in," the word *epichrio* refers to a physical "rubbing on." When Jesus anointed the eyes of the blind man, it was a physical "rubbing on" which resulted in a supernatural change. The man was not changed inwardly by that anointing, but outwardly.

When the *epichrio*, the anointing which comes on you and enables you to minister to others, is manifested in your life, you will feel the empowering presence of God. There is nothing quite like this experience, and it will change your life forever. You will feel like the prophet when he outran the chariots. You will feel as though you could carry the gates of the city off on your shoulders, as Samson did.

The Scriptures are full of powerful examples of men operating under a powerful *epichrio* anointing. When the Lord first approached Gideon, for instance, he was weak, frightened and unsure of himself. He was, in that very moment, hiding from his enemies. After God revealed His purpose for the young man, the Spirit of God came upon him, and he was supernaturally empowered to fulfill his call.

### GIVING WHAT YOU HAVE

Consider the case of Peter and John. They were walking along one day, on their way to the Temple to pray, when they came upon a lame man at the entrance of that holy spot. The man had been, according to the Scriptures, *"lame from his mother's womb"* (Acts 3:2). These two men, however, had an *epichrio* upon them. The Holy Spirit had come upon them, and they were just dripping with Holy Ghost oil, and ready to help somebody be free of burdens and yokes.

When the lame man caught their attention, and they realized that he was expecting to receive something from them, they began witnessing to him. Peter said, "I'm going to give you what I have." What he had was the anointing, the "rubbing on," the *epichrio*, and it was on him for the purpose of ministering to others.

When Peter told the lame man to rise and walk in the name of Jesus, the supernatural took over, and the lame man began *"walking and leaping and praising God"* (Verse 8). Peter had just demonstrated the *epichrio*, the anointing upon him for blessing others.

There is an eternal purpose for salvation and the anointing power of God in your life, and you have every reason to rejoice over that eternal purpose. But Jesus told us to *"occupy until [He] return[s]."* So, in the meantime, we must put to use the anointing He has placed on us for others.

## THE *EPICHRIO* IS FOR THE HERE AND NOW

Your *epichrio*, that anointing on you for others, will no longer be needed in Heaven. There will be no one to heal, because there will be no sickness there. No one will need to move in the prophetic gift there, because you will *"know even as [you] are known."* The *epichrio* is for the here and now. There is an earthly purpose for your being born again and anointed.

When the Holy Ghost has been poured on you, you must have the faith to hear when God speaks to you about ministry to others. Then you must have faith to seize the opportunities He presents for you to operate in His supernatural power to accomplish something for Him.

Isaiah prophesied (and Jesus fulfilled) the scriptures which said that the Spirit of God upon Jesus had anointed Him *"to preach the gospel to the poor,"* *"to heal the brokenhearted,"* *"to preach deliverance to the captives,"* and to bring *"recovering of sight to the blind,"* *"to set at liberty them that are bruised,"* *"to preach the acceptable year of the LORD"* (Luke 4:18). There was a purpose for His anointing.

It is the *epichrio* resting upon your life which allows you to witness with power, allows you to preach with conviction, and allows you to lay hands on the sick or bound and see supernatural results. When the Spirit of God comes upon you to do His work, it doesn't matter what circumstances you may face. You will be able to sing and praise and pray through any circumstances, because you feel that supernatural presence of God upon your life.

Just as the *enchrio* in you must be properly attended to so you can remain spiritually strong, the *epichrio* must be acted upon so that you can accomplish supernatural feats for God. It is this *epichrio* that gives you the ability to do, as Jesus promised you would, even *"greater works"* than He did (John 14:12).

## The Anointing upon You to Minister to Others

When that empowering presence of the *epichrio* comes upon you and works with the character-developing *enchrio* anointing in you, you can reach out in the power of the anointing and see burdens lifted and yokes destroyed. You will then demonstrate the reality of being *Empowered for the Call.*

# PART II:

# BIBLICAL FOUNDATIONS FOR THE ANOINTING

# SIX

# CHRIST, THE ANOINTED ONE

*He saith unto them, But whom say ye that I am?
And Simon Peter answered and said, THOU ART
THE CHRIST, the Son of the living God. And
Jesus answered and said unto him, Blessed art
thou, Simon Bar-jona: for flesh and blood hath not
revealed it unto thee, but my Father which is in
heaven.*                                Matthew 16:15-17

It would be absolutely impossible to study the
anointing without properly identifying Jesus Christ
for Who He really is. During His life on Earth those
who had no revelation of His divine origin called
Him *"Jesus of Nazareth"* or *"the carpenter's son."* Those
who really knew Him called Him the Christ, Jesus
Christ or Jesus the Christ .

Throughout the Scriptures, over and over again,
this term "Christ" is used, and most of the time we
read it like a name. Few people understand or acknowledge the significance of this exalted term.
Most of those who call themselves "Christians"

don't fully understand what they are saying when they use that word either.

"Christ" is the English transliteration of the Greek title *Christos*, which means "the Anointed One." "Christian" literally means "little christs" or "like Christ." So we are to be like Him. We are to bear the anointing of Him who is the Anointed One.

When Jesus began His ministry, something He taught or something He did made Him instantly famous throughout Galilee. The Scriptures record:

> *And he taught in their synagogues, being glori-fied of all.*                    Luke 4:15

What was it that caused people to *"glorify"* Jesus? The passage continues:

> *And he came to Nazareth, where he had been brought up: and, as his custom was, he went into the synagogue on the sabbath day, and stood up for to read. And there was delivered unto him the book of the prophet Esaias. And when he had opened the book, he found the place where it was written.*                    Luke 4:16-17

Jesus did not just pick a portion of scripture at random to read that day. The tradition in the synagogues of the first-century Galilee was that whoever read the scroll marked the place where he left off by inserting a pin, so that the next person to read could start at that point. Some previous reader in Nazareth had been led of the Spirit to stop reading precisely at the end of the sixtieth chapter of the prophecy of Isaiah, and when Jesus began reading, on the very next Sabbath, His words were these, later recounted by Luke:

> *The Spirit of the* LORD *is upon me, because he hath anointed me to preach the gospel to the poor; he hath sent me to heal the brokenhearted, to preach deliverance to the captives, and recovering of sight to the blind, to set at liberty them that are bruised, to preach the acceptable year of the Lord. And he closed the book, and he gave it again to the minister, and sat down. And the eyes of all them that were in the synagogue were fastened on him.*
>
> Luke 4:18-20

What Jesus was saying is that He was empowered for His call. The power of the Spirit was upon Him to fulfill the purpose of the Father that had been proclaimed by the prophets throughout many generations. Jesus had a mission and that mission was articulated in this passage. His call was to preach, heal, deliver, restore and liberate. He was supernaturally gifted to accomplish the fullness of that heavenly purpose.

Why did the people of Galilee glorify Him? Because to be anointed required Him to manifest the power that would fulfill His God-given purpose. The people of Galilee were healed, delivered, restored and liberated. The Anointed One backed His proclamation with a supernatural demonstration.

To be an anointed one, you must have an anointing. To be called, you must be empowered. So when you think of the title, Christ, you must think of His consecration, His call and the supernatural abilities He possessed to fulfill that call.

If you, the reader, would allow me the right to expand your thinking on that title, Christ, let us define it as the Anointed One (the Chosen One, the Called One) and His Anointing (the power and giftings which enabled Him to carry out that call).

If we could reread the Bible with a new revelation of who Christ really was and is, and every time we come upon the word "Christ" substitute the words "the Anointed One and His Anointing (power and giftings)," it would revolutionize our lives. For example: *"I can do all things through Christ which strengthens me"* (Philippians 4:13) literally means *"I can do all things through the Anointed One and His Anointing (power and giftings) Who strengthens me."*

When Paul taught: *"Follow me as I follow Christ,"* he literally meant: *"Follow me as I follow the Anointed One and His Anointing (power and giftings)."*

The man that history knows as Jesus of Nazareth was and is the Christ, the Anointed One and His Anointing (power and giftings), yet He was unable to do many great miracles in His own hometown. The people there could not look beyond their knowledge of His humble birth and natural parentage to see God's hand upon Him and the anointing that made Him uniquely the Anointed One.

Peter, a man from another town in Galilee, received the revelation of Who Jesus really was. When Jesus asked His disciples, *"Who do men say that I am?"* some of them answered, *"Isaiah,"* and some *"Elijah,"* but Peter answered, *"Thou art the Christ [the Anointed One and His Anointing (power and giftings)], the Son of the living God."*

Jesus responded, *"Blessed art thou, Simon Bar-jona: for flesh and blood hath not revealed it unto thee, but my Father which is in Heaven."* He went on to say to His disciple:

> *And I say also unto thee, That thou art Peter, and upon this rock I will build my church; and the gates of hell shall not prevail against it. And I will give unto thee the keys of the kingdom of heaven: and whatsoever thou shalt bind on earth shall be bound in heaven: and whatsoever thou shalt loose on earth shall be loosed in heaven.*
>
> Matthew 16:18-19

### THE ROCK OF REVELATION

The Church, thus, was built upon the rock of the revelation of the Anointed One. The foundation of the entire Kingdom of God would be the revelation that Jesus was more than a carpenter's son, more than just another prophet or teacher. He is the Son of the living God. He is the Anointed One.

The Church is built upon the revelation of who Jesus is and upon the power He possessed. When we, therefore, have a revelation of His true identity and the fullness of His power, we possess the very revelation that birthed and built the Church.

When you read the scriptural words, *"Christ in you the hope of glory,"* you can now recognize what it really means, and you will rejoice, knowing that it literally promises that the Anointed One and His Anointing (power and giftings) is in you. That fact is your *"hope of glory."* You are *Empowered for the Call.*

# CHAPTER

## SEVEN

# THE GOSPEL OF THE ANOINTING

*And this GOSPEL OF THE KINGDOM shall
be preached in all the world for a witness unto all
nations; and then shall the end come.*

Matthew 24:14

As believers, we have been given by our Lord the
Great Commission. We are to *"go ... into all the world,
and preach the Gospel."* But what does that really en-
tail? What does it mean to each of us personally?
What is it that we are to share with others?

The very foundation of the Kingdom of God is
the revelation that Jesus was more than just another
man. He was the Son of the Living God, the
Anointed One and His Anointing (power and
giftings). The word "gospel" means "good news,"
and the "good news" that Jesus proclaimed when
He showed that He was the fulfillment of the prophecy of Isaiah was that He was indeed the One
anointed by God to remove burdens and destroy
yokes. It is our assignment, then, to carry forth the

good news that Jesus Christ is the Anointed One and His Anointing (power and giftings).

There is more to our calling than that. Consider Jesus' words as recorded in the final chapter of Mark:

> *And these signs shall follow them that believe; In my name shall they cast out devils; they shall speak with new tongues; They shall take up serpents; and if they drink any deadly thing, it shall not hurt them; they shall lay hands on the sick, and they shall recover.*　　　　Mark 16:17-18

It is only after we have the true revelation of the anointing in us for us that we can accomplish the Great Commission in its fullness. That is when we are able to operate in the power, authority, favor, holiness and virtue that will demonstrate, through us, all that Jesus Christ truly is.

## WHAT BEING A "CHRISTIAN" REALLY MEANS

Being a Christian does not just mean that you are a follower of Christ. It means you are like Him. It means you are anointed like Him, and you have what He has. The believers were first called "Christians" in Antioch after Paul and Barnabas had been there preaching. So what were they preaching? They were preaching the burden-removing, yoke-destroying power of God. Those who came in sick to their services left healed, and those who came in bound left free. That was why the early members of the Church were called "Christians." They were operating in the anointing of the Anointed One.

Our demonstration of power must not be less powerful than theirs, for the Lord is anointing His Body in these end-times to fulfill His Commission, to put forth His message, the message of the Anointed One. The anointing, therefore, *is* the message of the day.

Of course we must preach salvation, repentance and the love of God, but our message must go far beyond that. The message of this hour must not be one that only touches minds and emotions. It must be a message that removes burdens and destroys yokes. Let it be a message to loose the power, the authority, the favor, the holiness and the virtue of God upon the lives of His people.

### EXPOUNDING *"MORE PERFECTLY"*

Luke, the writer of the Acts of the Apostles, related the story of a preacher named Apollos. He was described as a Jew and *"an eloquent man, mighty in the Scriptures"* (Acts 18:24). He went to Ephesus and there was instructed himself *"more fully"* in the way of the Lord, because he had known only the baptism of John.

His instructors, Aquila and Priscilla, had been

with Paul and had heard Him preaching the Gospel of the anointing. When they heard Apollos preach, they took him aside and *"expounded unto him the way of God more perfectly"* (Verses 26). After that, Apollos went on to Achaia, and began teaching that Jesus was the Christ, the Anointed One.

This is an important message for our time as well, but we seem to have a whole generation of Apolloses, those who are about a message behind what God is trying to speak right now. Those who have learned the *"more perfect"* way, the truth of the Gospel of the Anointed One, need to step forth in the fullness of that anointing. It is time for the believers of today to take the bold stand that Paul took:

*And my speech and my preaching was not with enticing words of man's wisdom, but in demonstration of the Spirit and of power:*

1 Corinthians 2:4

*For I am not ashamed of the gospel of Christ: for it is the power of God unto salvation.*

Romans 1:16

Paul was not ashamed of the Good News of the Anointed One, and he was bold to demonstrate the power of that anointing. He had conceived the revelation, gone through his time of preparation, and was actively accessing his anointing of destination, thus fulfilling the call God had placed on his life.

# The Gospel of the Anointing

## TRANSFORMING MINDS

Too many preachers today are trying to appeal to flesh. They are trying to intellectualize, rationalize and get through to people's brains and emotions. It's time for them to realize that you *cannot* get through to people's brains because their minds are burdened and yoked and must be transformed. The only thing that can remove those burdens and destroy those yokes is the anointing. This is the message with which we have been entrusted, and this is the message we must preach, whether people like it or not:

> *But as we were allowed of God to be put in trust with the gospel, even so we speak; not as pleasing men, but God, which trieth our hearts.*
>
> 1 Thessalonians 2:4

The message that must be preached these days is the Gospel of the Kingdom, the Gospel of doing things God's way. That is the Gospel of the anointing. When you preach the Good News of God's Kingdom and anointing, the yokes of sin, disease, depression and satanic oppression are destroyed. It is for this reason that God has entrusted to us His great power. This is the reason we have been *Empowered for the Call.*

# EIGHT

# THE ANOINTING IN OLD TESTAMENT TIMES

*And the spirit of the LORD will come upon thee, and thou shalt prophesy with them, and shalt be turned into another man. And let it be, when these signs are come unto thee, that thou do as occasion serve thee; for God is with thee.*

1 Samuel 10:6-7

Throughout the Bible we can see examples of God's anointing power being poured out on men and women. Long before Jesus made his declaration of being the Anointed One, and long before God gave Peter the revelation of the importance of the Anointed One and His Anointing (power and giftings), Old Testament men and women were anointed for specific tasks by God. It came to be understood in Old Testament times that the physical anointing of a person by the prophets was a significant step in the bestowal of power and authority from on high.

## *Empowered for the Call*

### SAUL AND DAVID WERE ANOINTED

The record of Saul's physical anointing contains the revelation of what is, doubtless, one of the most important factors of the spiritual anointing — the tangible and visible transformation in a person when the anointing power of God is upon him. Saul was *"turned into another man."* That doesn't mean that Saul felt "special," nor that he began behaving a little differently. He was literally *"turned into another man."* The anointing changes everything, so much so that an anointed person seems to no longer be the same person at all. This is important, because we cannot do God's work in our own abilities.

There is nothing in your carnal nature capable of breaking bondages and changing lives. So, for the anointing to be effective in your life and ministry, you must be willing to be turned into a completely new person.

When he was anointed, young Saul suddenly became a gifted prophet. One minute he had been trailing after his father's lost asses, and the next minute he was speaking forth the mysteries of God. That doesn't happen outside of the anointing.

Because God had chosen Saul to be *"captain over His inheritance,"* He gave him favor and empowered him from that day forward with a burden-removing, yoke-destroying kingly authority. Everyone around him knew it, too, for there was a visible change in him.

# The Anointing in Old Testament Times

David was anointed in a similar way:

*Then Samuel took the horn of oil, and anointed him in the midst of his brethren: and the spirit of the LORD came upon David from that day forward.*
                                                1 Samuel 16:13

Most people are familiar with the story of how Samuel was led to the house of Jesse to find and anoint the next king of Israel from among his sons. As each son was presented to the prophet, each in turn was rejected, until it seemed there were no more sons to present. The family had purposely left out the one son whom God had chosen. Because David seemed insignificant to them, he was left in the fields, tending the sheep. No one had bothered to call him. After all, he was only a shepherd boy.

This story teaches another powerful and basic truth about the anointing power of God. It is a sovereign gift of God; and our natural, carnal reasoning, our personal sense of value or worth, or what others think of us, has absolutely nothing to do with it. David's experience underscores the fact that it is not our education or our natural talents or abilities, nor our age or recognized accomplishments which make us eligible for the anointing power of God to be made manifest in our lives. The empowerment of our call is a sovereign gift from God to enable us to fulfill His purpose for His glory.

Among all the valuable lessons which can be learned from the scriptural record of the anointing of Saul and David, another stands out. God has a sovereign timing to be taken into consideration. Saul stepped into his kingly authority immediately, but David had to wait many years. He was anointed to be king from a very young age, but God delayed his anointing of destination for a very long time. In neither case was it the choice of the man involved. God chooses the time.

After you have received your anointing of revelation and have chosen to obey God, it is not your choice as to whether or not the fullness of that anointing manifests itself immediately or much later. Some calls require longer periods of preparation than others. We must leave that choice with God, for He knows best.

Another key found in the story of these first two kings of Israel is in recognizing the importance of maintaining the *enchrio*, the anointing in you for your own edification. If we are to successfully fulfill our call, we must keep our personal lives under the anointing power of God.

When David was anointed, Saul was still king. Because Saul had grown lax and hardened, however, and had allowed his position of authority to go to his head, he had begun to play with the anointing of God, to take it for granted. This put his power in jeopardy.

## The Anointing in Old Testament Times

Saul's culminating sin, failing to destroy the Amalekites, may not seem like such a serious offense. God, however, had specifically commanded him to destroy them, so the failure to do so represented rebellion against the Lord Himself. This resulted in Saul ultimately losing his anointing and being turned over to an evil spirit.

Years later, David sinned against God, too, when he committed adultery with Bathsheba and murdered her husband to try to cover up his failing. Rather than being cut off and forgotten, however, David was remembered as *"a man after [God's] own heart"* (1 Samuel 13:14).

What was the difference between the two cases? Shortly after Saul had sinned, God sent Samuel to him to point out his wrong, to give him an opportunity to repent and put himself back in right relationship with God. Saul refused to admit his wrongdoing and was blatantly unrepentant.

After David sinned, God sent Nathan to point out to the king the error of his ways. David's reaction was just the opposite of Saul's. He made no excuses, blamed no one but himself, and repented immediately.

Both men paid a dear price for their sins, but the one — through heartfelt repentance — was able to keep a good relationship with the Lord and to continue walking in the empowerment of his anointing to fulfill his call. Somehow David had been able to understand the revelation of the importance of maintaining the *enchrio* in order to continue operating in the *epichrio*.

Maintaining the *enchrio* was what made it possible for David to simply cut off a piece of Saul's garment and take it with him, when he had the opportunity to kill his adversary. Although he was not a perfect man in any sense of the word, he had died sufficiently to his carnal nature, as to not want revenge on the man who had been threatening his life and causing him such misery. The anointing upon his personal life was real, as well as his anointing of preparation to be king. Therefore, he walked not only in power and authority, but also in the holiness and virtue of that *enchrio* anointing.

I am fully convinced that God's anointing power would be manifested in far greater degree in the Church today if anointed men and women would learn to walk in repentance and integrity, maintaining a right relationship with God and keeping their *enchrio* fresh.

### Joshua and Caleb Were Anointed

Another startling case is that of Joshua, the man who took Moses' place. He had learned how to open himself up to the Spirit of God and how to allow God to pour into him His glory, and was chosen for such an important position because he had developed a relationship with God, and allowed God to mold his spirit. This attitude pleased God and caused Him to mark Joshua for greater things. When you are faithful to attend to the deposit God has made in you for you, you can lay hold of an anointing for the people.

Since Moses was still living when God chose Joshua, there was not an immediate full release of God's power on his life. He had to await the timing of God for him to step forth in all authority. Some people chafe under the timing of God, but that's foolish. We must each learn to wait for that perfect timing. God has a very specific purpose for our lives, just as He did for Joshua. Leave the timing of your rise to full prominence to God, trusting that He knows what He is doing.

There was something obviously different about Joshua's life. He was a man of the *enchrio*. There was a visible and undeniable power, authority, favor, holiness and virtue upon him. But God knew that Joshua needed even more. Because the task ahead of him was so great, Joshua would need unusual wisdom and power. Therefore, God led Moses to anoint Joshua again. This new anointing was not so much for Joshua's sake as it was for the people's. He must have their confidence if he was to complete his call and lead God's people to victory in the Promised Land.

When Moses sent the twelve spies into the Promised Land to scout out the land, ten of them returned convinced that it was impossible to take the land. Forgetting the fact that God had promised them the land, those ten men insisted that they were as helpless as grasshoppers against the resident giants.

Joshua was one of the twelve entrusted with this task of spying out the land, and his impression was altogether different from that of the ten. Here he showed his true colors, the evidence of the anointing upon his life. He knew they were able to take the land because God had said so.

Joshua was not the only one who stood his ground and trusted God's promises in the face of adverse circumstances. There was a second anointed spy — Caleb. What made the difference in the lives of these two spies is so simple that it seems hard to believe. Joshua and Caleb had a different spirit ruling them. Something had so changed them that they thought, spoke and acted differently than their peers.

The ten spies who were practical and logical were being ruled by a spirit of fear, and God cannot honor fear. Because Joshua and Caleb operated in faith in God's promises rather than fear, they reacted to the identical circumstances with calmness, dignity and assurance. God could and did honor their faith-filled reaction. He said of Caleb:

*But my servant Caleb, because he had another spirit with him, and hath followed me fully, him*

*will I bring into the land whereinto he went; and
his seed shall possess it.*          Numbers 14:24

While the ten disgruntled spies played with God
and found themselves robbed of God's very best,
Joshua and Caleb and their descendants went on to
possess the land and to have all that God wanted
for them.

Our God is *"the same, yesterday and today and for
ever"* (Hebrews 13:8). He still cannot honor fear, but
He will honor that confidence that comes from an
*enchrio* built on a right relationship with Him. He
wants you to accept all the promises of His anointing power and possess all He has for you and your
seed.

### QUEEN ESTHER AND OTHERS WERE ANOINTED

Esther was given favor from God to prepare her
for the anointing of power she would need to fulfill
her call — even before she knew what her assignment was. The Scriptures declare:

*And Esther obtained favour in the sight of all them
that looked upon her.*          Esther 2:15

God provided Mordecai to stand alongside Esther, to encourage her to fulfill her destiny and to
keep her on track. Similarly, God provided Deborah,

already anointed as a prophetess, to get Barak moving to fulfill the calling God had given him to overcome his enemies. Aaron was anointed to be at Moses' side, to shore him up in his moment's of weakness.

From the beginning of the Old Testament to the end, God showed the greatness of what He desires to do through anointed people, and this is the will of God for you and me today. Despite all your limitations, you are *Empowered for the Call.*

# Chapter

---

## Nine

# Joseph's Anointed Lifestyle

*And Joseph was brought down to Egypt; and Potiphar, an officer of Pharaoh, captain of the guard, an Egyptian, bought him of the hands of the Ishmeelites, which had brought him down thither. And THE LORD WAS WITH JOSEPH, and he was a prosperous man; and he was in the house of his master the Egyptian. And his master saw that the LORD was with him, and that the LORD made all that he did to prosper in his hand.*

Genesis 39:1-3

No study of the anointing power of God upon men and women would be complete without a reference to the man I consider to be one of the best examples of anointed lifestyle in the Bible — Joseph. Virtually all elements and aspects of the anointing power of God are illustrated in this one extraordinary life.

God has dealt with me so forcefully from the life of Joseph, and I have been led to preach so extensively from his life that it would take another book to explore fully what I feel about him and his anointing. Here, at least, I want to consider some of the highlights.

Joseph was literally born with supernatural favor on his life, and that God-given favor met with opposition from the very beginning. This is important to note because as you step into the favor of God, you will not necessarily win any popularity contests with the world.

To make matters worse, when Joseph had a dream that revealed to him his eventual anointing to be leader over his people, in his innocence he shared that dream with his brothers. He had received this revelation deep into his spirit, and it made such a lasting impression on him that he would never forget it (although the evidence of its fulfillment was nowhere in sight). The very thought, however, infuriated his brothers and caused them to decide to destroy him.

Joseph had nothing to worry about. Although the enemy will always try his best to destroy our anointing, he cannot overpower the favor of God that comes upon us as a result of that anointing. As long as we keep the *enchrio* fresh upon us, there is nothing man or demon can do to stop us.

The brothers intended for Joseph to die of exposure in a deep pit, but God had another plan, one that would prepare Joseph for his anointing of destination, and that plan took precedence over the enemy's plan of destruction. From the moment they put Joseph into that pit, the brothers began to assume that Joseph was out of the picture, but God was positioning their younger brother to rule, and wherever he went he would prosper.

The difficult circumstances of being sold into servitude did not discourage Joseph, and God continued to grant him power, authority, and honor. Joseph recognized the importance of maintaining his relationship with God, whatever happened, and his *enchrio* did not diminish, but continued to grow.

Before long, we see evident in the life of Joseph in Egypt the very nature of God, His holiness, His character. Joseph was a man of virtue, and when the wife of his master set a trap for him and tried to seduce him, he was able to resist her. His decision to risk angering his master's wife was based on his deep conviction of God's plan for his future. He said:

> *How then can I do this great wickedness, and sin against God?* Genesis 39:9

What happened next doesn't seem to be a very happy conclusion to the matter. Joseph was falsely accused of attacking his master's wife and thrown into prison. Despite these difficult circumstances, however, Joseph remained true to his calling. He knew that God had a plan for him bigger than his prison cell, and he clung to that revelation. This seemingly tragic event, therefore, was not able to destroy the anointing upon the young man's life. Clinging to the prophetic revelation of the calling for which God has anointed you is the thing that will enable you to remain free in your spirit, even during the most confining and unpleasant of experiences.

Because of his loyalty to his calling, Joseph was able to continue operating in his anointing during his physical confinement. If he had withdrawn into himself and dwelt on the wrongs done to him, he might never have come out of that prison alive. But Joseph did not allow the circumstances, difficult as they were, to overwhelm and discourage him or to stop him from obeying God and doing the works of the Lord. His care to maintain his *enchrio* anointing through a continued relationship with God caused him to have an *epichrio* anointing which he was able to exercise in his interpretation of dreams for the other prisoners. This not only provided prophetic words for the others, but was the key to Joseph's subsequent release and promotion.

When you have an anointing of God operating in your life, you dare not let even the most dire circumstances around you discourage you from stepping forth to do what God requests. What may, at the time, seem like an exercise in frustration in the natural may well be the exercise of preparation. Trust that God is preparing you to move to the next level of your anointing.

When God's time was right, He arranged for Joseph to interpret the dreams for Pharaoh that resulted in him being placed as second in command in Egypt. This was what Joseph had seen in his dream as a teenager, yet it had taken many years — years of seeming turmoil — to bring him to this point. Now his natural position reflected his spiritual condition of power, authority and favor, but he had seen it years earlier through the revelation of God.

## A Very Different Test

Now Joseph faced a very different kind of test. How would he treat the brothers who had betrayed him? He had been raised up by God to save them, but could he now find it in his heart to return good to those who had shown him nothing but evil?

If Joseph had failed at this point, he might never have become a household name, but he did not fail. The godly character he had maintained throughout all his natural ups and downs now manifested itself again. God's holiness and virtue were evident in his decisions now regarding his brothers, and he returned them good and not evil.

Because Joseph was obedient and in right relationship with God, and because he clung to his prophetic promises when everything seemed to be lost, God was able to use him to deliver the Israelites from starvation and to position them in the land He had chosen for them. Joseph's obedience to God's call and his patience to wait for God's timing allowed prophetic promises to be fulfilled for both natural and spiritual Israel.

Could Joseph have understood as a young man what an important part in the history of his nation and other nations he would play? Probably not. All he knew was that God had anointed him and that he had a leadership role ahead of him. That was enough, however. He accepted that revelation and placed it so deeply within his spirit that it drove him to seek an ever-closer relationship with God and to maintain the vision of his calling through every circumstance. He was willing to trust God to do whatever was necessary to bring His Word to pass. As the wise writer of Proverbs advised:

> *Trust in the* LORD *with all thine heart; and lean not unto thine own understanding. In all thy ways acknowledge him, and he shall direct thy paths.*
> Proverbs 3:5-6

The lifestyle of Joseph shows us that when a young man receives a revelation of his destiny and yields himself to the preparation necessary to fulfill that destiny, he will ultimately arrive at his God-appointed destination. Because the issues of character and holiness were always in proper order in Joseph's life, when it was time for God to promote him, the power He placed on Joseph's life loosed favor and the favor loosed a recognized authority. In Joseph's life, therefore, we find a blueprint for the anointed lifestyle God desires for each of us. In the following section we will examine the five dynamics of the anointing that enabled Joseph to fulfill the call of God upon his life.

Like Joseph, you have no idea what the potential importance and impact of your anointing on spiritual and natural history might be in these last days of time. You are *Empowered for the Call.*

# PART III:

# THE FIVE DYNAMICS OF THE ANOINTING

# THE ENDUEMENT OF POWER

*But YE SHALL RECEIVE POWER, after that the Holy Ghost is come upon you: and ye shall be witnesses unto me both in Jerusalem, and in all Judaea, and in Samaria, and unto the uttermost part of the earth.* Acts 1:8

When the Lord calls you to accomplish some specific task for His glory, He also gives you the power to fulfill that call. As soon as you conceive the anointing of revelation, you receive a transferring or impartation of His power made available to you, so that you can prepare to step into your destiny in God.

Paul wrote:

*Finally, my brethren, be strong in the Lord, and in the power of his might.* Ephesians 6:10

Your strength to accomplish something for God

is not something you can conjure up in your flesh, no matter how much you might desire it. It is only in *"the power of His might"* that you can truly do anything worthwhile. It is only *"after that the Holy Ghost [has] come upon you"* that *"ye shall receive power"* to *"be witnesses."* Like the early apostles, to become effective you must operate in the anointing:.

> *And with great power gave the apostles witness of the resurrection of the Lord Jesus: and great grace was upon them all.* Acts 4:33

When you have accepted this enduement of power and determined to step forth to do the works of God, you will quickly see the benefits of that power, not only in the lives of those to whom you minister, but in your own life as well:

> *Behold, I give unto you power to tread on serpents and scorpions, and over all the power of the enemy: and nothing shall by any means hurt you.* Luke 10:19

It is the supernatural power of God, bestowed on you as God's anointed vessel, that makes you capable of facing every enemy head-on, confident of the promise: *"greater is He that is in you, than He that is in the world"* (1 John 4:4).

# The Enduement of Power

Your aim is to be like Jesus, to manifest the Anointed One  and His Anointing (power and giftings) to the world. Therefore, you must step forth in the power with which He has gifted you to manifest His signs and wonders. You will see the sick healed, the blind eyes opened, the burdens removed and the yokes destroyed — just as He did.

The key to seeing the lost coming to Jesus will be a manifestation of the power of the Holy Ghost. The disciples were commanded to tarry in Jerusalem until they received power. They did not become competent witnesses until the *dunamis*, which is the power of God or the divine abilities of God, was truly upon them. The world must be convinced that God is real,  and it is the power of the Holy Ghost that will provide us with the evidence that the message we preach is the truth.

In Joseph's case, there were two distinct giftings or divine empowerments that flowed from his life: prophetic dreams (and the ability to interpret prophetic dreams) and a God-given ability to administrate. These gifts opened the door for  God to then loose authority upon Joseph's life.

As God's power is made evident in your life and ministry, you will elicit the same response that Jesus did when He manifested God's power to the world:

*But when the multitudes saw it, they marvelled,*

*and glorified God, which had given such power
unto men.* Matthew 9:8

God has great things in store for your life, so don't
be afraid to believe Him for greatness. You are
anointed. You are *Empowered for the Call.*

# ELEVEN

# AUTHORITY FROM GOD

*And I will give unto thee THE KEYS OF THE KINGDOM of heaven: and whatsoever thou shalt bind on earth shall be bound in heaven: and whatsoever thou shalt loose on earth shall be loosed in heaven.*                    Matthew 16:19

As wonderful as it is to recognize that God has given you power to manifest His works, that is only the beginning of what He wants to do to equip you as you go forth to fulfill His call on your life. He also wants to give you authority.

There was a time when I considered the two things, power and authority, to be one and the same. After all, doesn't the one bring the other? Then the Lord began to deal with me and show me the difference between these two gifts.

When you have power, there is a small territory in which that particular power works. You might think of it as a small circle. If you have a prophetic gift, there is an empowerment in a small circle in which you prophesy. If you have the gift of working miracles, there is a power in you to work miracles, another small circle.

## AUTHORITY ENCOMPASSES MANY AREAS

When you are anointed of God, you have power for specific things (those small circles of empowerment), but He also gives you a greater authority. This greater authority is like a much larger circle that encompasses those other smaller circles and much more. The authority that comes from God with His power will impact many additional dynamics of your life.

One reason that the church today does not operate at the level of effectiveness that it should is that too many people are content to settle for just power. If they can have an occasional healing or an occasional manifestation of one of the other gifts, they are satisfied. Too many are settling for mere power, when God wants to give them authority.

The keys given to Peter represent authority, the authority to bind and loose. Somewhere along the line the church has laid down the keys and relinquished its God-given authority.

When Samuel anointed Saul as king over Israel, he told him he had been chosen *"captain over the Lord's inheritance."* When you walk in a kingly-type anointing, you are walking in an anointing of authority. An anointing of authority means that you are moving into a place of ruling and reigning in the spiritual realm. You become empowered to rule and reign over spiritual issues in your own life and in the lives of others as well.

When you operate under the anointing of authority, you become responsible to attend to the things which affect the future of the Kingdom of God.

### RECOGNITION OF AUTHORITY

When God chose Joshua to succeed Moses as the leader of the children of Israel, it was because He saw a different spirit within him. When Moses laid his hands on Joshua and imparted God's authority to him, it was not a man-made promotion. It was the God-granted passing along of a God-given authority. It was only because he manifested this God-given authority that Joshua could step into such an important position and lead such a large group of people. They recognized the authority of God in operation in him. When you step into God-given authority, those around you will recognize that authority. God has promised that He will make *"even [your] enemies to be at peace with [you]"* (Proverbs 16:7).

Pharaoh's people threw Joseph in jail. Yet in the end, it was Pharaoh who, although he didn't understand it, was moved by the power (giftedness) of Joseph's life. Something about this man Joseph impressed even the Pharaoh and his servants:

*And Pharaoh said unto his servants, Can we find
such a one as this is, a man in whom the Spirit of
God is?*                                      Genesis 41:38

It was after Joseph manifested his God-given power that he found favor with the Pharaoh and was moved into that position of natural authority.

Many people are afraid to exercise the gifts they already have and, therefore, cannot move into greater authority. If Joseph had been afraid to use the gifts given to him by God for fear of angering the Pharaoh, he would not have been promoted to the strategic position to which he ascended. When we are given authority, we must be bold to do what our position demands. If Joseph had been afraid to use the authority given to him by Pharaoh, he would not have gotten very far. We cannot hold back in fear of what others will say about the exercise of our authority. We must make proper use of it, even if we meet with the displeasure of men.

The choice is yours. You can walk around like a prisoner or you can walk around like a man who has the keys to the Kingdom in his pocket.

## AUTHORITY OVER SATAN

Satan and his evil spirits recognize and must bow to the authority of God, and it is when you begin operating in the God-given authority of your anointing that you are able to put the devil in his place under your feet. One story in the New Testament expresses this quite well:

> *Then certain of the vagabond Jews, exorcists, took upon them to call over them which had evil spirits the name of the Lord Jesus, saying, We adjure you by Jesus whom Paul preacheth. And there were seven sons of one Sceva, a Jew, and chief of the priests, which did so. And the evil spirit answered and said, Jesus I know, and Paul I know; but who are ye?* Acts 19:13-15

In the end, the evil spirits jumped on the seven sons of Sceva, beat them, stripped them, and sent them running. The demons knew the authority of Jesus and the authority of Paul, and they respected it, but they had no respect for these other men.

Demons will respect you when you operate in God-given authority, but anyone who attempts to stand against demon forces without the authority of the anointing of God is just asking for trouble. You'll be defeated every time. It is only when you have submitted yourself to God and allowed His authority to operate in your life that you can obey the words of the Scriptures:

> *Resist the devil, and he will flee from you.*
> James 4:7

When a man is faithful to use the power of God in obedience to the Holy Spirit, he is positioning himself for promotion that will enlarge his territory of responsibility. God desires you to have victory in all areas — physically, emotionally, spiritually, financially and relationally.

Joseph was faithful not to allow bitter disappointments to quench the flow of God's power, and he, therefore, became a candidate for the promotion of the Lord.

You, too, can be promoted from the place of power to the position of authority. You are *Empowered for the Call.*

# THE BESTOWAL OF FAVOR

*For whoso findeth me findeth life, and SHALL
OBTAIN FAVOUR of the LORD.*

Proverbs 8:35

When you are anointed, you know you are
anointed, and have experienced the power and authority of God in your life, you should expect the
bestowal of His favor. He has promised it.

While favor is one of the basic dynamics of the
anointing, it does not come without preparation.
Jesus, the Anointed One, is your model for every
part of your life, and even His favor with God was
the result of preparation:

*And Jesus increased in wisdom and stature, and
in favour with God and man.*          Luke 2:52

The increase of favor is not automatic or instan-
taneous. It comes over a period of time as you prove
yourself faithful. God wants to know that He can

trust you to use His favor properly. If you stay long enough in the presence of God, the change in your life will become noticeable.

Why did Jesus favor Peter, James and John? It was because they stayed closer to Him than others. They continually sought His presence and were always eager for His teachings. Jesus did not choose to favor them over the other disciples. It was rather they who chose Him more than the others, and the result was that they were blessed with favor.

When you are favored of God, it becomes obvious. Others may not understand it, but they will be able to see the favor God bestows on you. Of the children of Israel, God said:

*And I will give this people favour in the sight of the Egyptians: and it shall come to pass, that, when ye go, ye shall not go empty.* Exodus 3:21

The Egyptians despised the Israelites and were hard taskmasters over them. There was no way they wanted to see them prosper. But when God has declared a thing, nothing that Satan can do will stop it. God said that the Israelites would have favor with the Egyptians, and they did.

The Egyptians must have wondered why they were blessing the Israelites, when they had always despised them. But God knew what He was doing and gave the people favor in the sight of their oppressors.

# The Bestowal of Favor

## FAVOR OUTWEIGHS ANY CIRCUMSTANCE

In order to give Joseph favor in prison, God had to change the heart of the pagan jailer. When you allow the anointing of God to flow through you, God can give you favor that seems impossible in the natural.

Every man or woman of faith we read about in the Bible had battles, tribulations and afflictions, but these people also had God's favor. He has promised that *"where sin abounded, grace did much more abound"* (Romans 5:20). When the attack of the enemy comes, the favor of God will be even greater on your life — as long as you remain faithful to Him and hold fast to the anointing with which He has gifted you.

If you know you are anointed of God and have not yet experienced His favor, continue to use the gifts God has deposited in your life. Circumstances mean nothing. You can look beyond circumstances because God is with you. The devil wants you to stop doing what you are anointed to do. By faith you can walk through *the valley of the shadow of death*, but if you lay down in the fire you will be burnt beyond recognition.

While Joseph was in prison, he continued to exercise his gift. He offered help to the king's butler and the king's cupbearer. He asked them to remember him when they were released. When they didn't,

Joseph still refused to be discouraged. He would not allow his anointing to be quenched. He was learning that true favor never comes from man; it comes from God. When the time was right, God took care of Joseph:

> *And Pharaoh took off his ring from his hand, and put it upon Joseph's hand, and arrayed him in vestures of fine linen, and put a gold chain about his neck. And he made him to ride in the second chariot which he had; and they cried before him, Bow the knee: and he made him ruler over all the land of Egypt. And Pharaoh said unto Joseph, I am Pharaoh, and without thee shall no man lift up his hand or foot in all the land of Egypt.*
>
> Genesis 41:42-44

That is the kind of favor only God can supply, and it comes with our faithfulness to the anointing. This favor is not something you must earn. It is a gift from God that He bestows lovingly and gladly. He said to His disciples:

> *Fear not, little flock; for it is your Father's good pleasure to give you the kingdom.*    Luke 12:32

So, if you are an anointed vessel of God, expect His favor on your life. You have power, you have authority, and you have favor. You are unique, handmade and custom-crafted to do a work for God. You are destined to have favor with men — wherever you happen to go. As someone walking around with the burden-removing, yoke-destroying anointing of God on your life, you will find that people will sometimes bless you and not even understand why. Don't try to figure it out. Just enjoy the gift of God.

If you are a member of the business community, expect to find favor in business. God wants to be with you when you negotiate a business contract or buy a house or a car. He wants to give you favor with those with whom you are dealing on a regular basis.

If you are part of the educational community, expect to be honored. You are favored of the Lord.

Favor is a benefit of your anointing, but it is also a tool to be used to further the work of the Lord. When you are in a position of favor, you are in a position to be effective. The favor that God gave Joseph was not just for his own benefit. It was a strategic part of God's plan to position Joseph and ultimately bless His people.

Enjoy your favor, but always look for ways to allow God to use it — as an opportunity to testify of the goodness of your God and an opening to manifest the burden-removing, yoke-destroying power you possess.

When Joseph refused to allow negative circumstances to quench his giftedness, he posititioned himself for a bestowal of favor that resulted in a promotion to authority. Determine to be like Joseph, for you are *Empowered for the Call.*

# THE IMPARTATION OF HOLINESS

*And thou shalt make a plate of pure gold, and grave upon it, like the engravings of a signet, HOLINESS TO THE LORD.* Exodus 28:36

Holiness is not a popular subject these days. Many pastors have come to avoid preaching and teaching on it because they don't want to frighten people away from their church. This, however, is an important subject, *"without which no man shall see the Lord."*

There is more to being like the Lord than laying hands on the sick, speaking in tongues or praying for the oppressed. Those are manifestations of power, but God has an anointing of holiness He wants to manifest in our lives. The anointing of holiness is an anointing of purity and godliness or Godlikeness.

Many tend to think that while the power and the gifts come from God, holiness must come from within us. The truth is that we have no holiness of our own. There is no holiness to be found in us apart from *His* holiness. Only God is holy, and He is the source of all things holy. So, if we want holiness, we must go to the Source.

God is holiness, so the closer you get to Him, the more you live in Him, the more you move in Him and have your being in Him, the more holy you will become. It will be because of Him, not because of you. It will be because being with Him, you will have become conformed to His image.

## THE RELATIONSHIP BREAKS THE BONDAGE

Many churches name all the things that are un-holy and tell their members to get holy by dropping those things from their lives. They may be able to drop some things on their own, but that's not true holiness. You could live with that self-generated holiness and still be on your way to Hell. You might look clean on the outside, but the inside would still be dirty. You might still continue to sin and just look differently while you were doing it.

A pastor might tell his people that smoking is harmful and dirty and that they shouldn't do it, and some may heed his words and stop smoking. But if those same people could get into a relationship with God and let Him speak to them on the subject, true holiness would come forth from their lives before long.

## The Impartation of Holiness

When you get into an intimate relationship with God, no one has to tell you not to sniff something into your nose, shoot something into your veins, or pour something from a bottle to give you an artificial high. You don't need a sermon spelling out the evils of crack cocaine, heroine or marijuana. You know instinctively that these things are not of God and gladly walk away from them, recognizing them for the bondage they represent.

Some people might say, "But it's not easy to give up these habits," and they have a point — if they are speaking of giving these things up on their own accord. Doing it in the flesh is not easy, and many fail, as so many others before them have.

If your motive for desiring holiness is wrong, you will fail, and if your method is wrong, you will fail, too. It is only when your desire for holiness in your life is based on your relationship with the Lord and your desire to deepen that relationship that you will succeed. Then you don't have to do it by yourself. He will do it for you.

### The Anointing Imparts Holiness

You may ask, "How does the anointing impart holiness?" If the law of the anointing is true, then the person in whom the anointing resides is able to remove burdens and destroy yokes. The things in your life that make you ungodly or unholy cannot be destroyed by the power of the flesh, mind or emotions. The deliverance must come through the power of the Holy Ghost.

When you walk as a vessel open to the presence of God, the anointing of the Lord continually deals with the areas of your life that would draw you away from His presence.

How could Joseph resist the temptation of Potiphar's wife when his mind knew it would result in dismissal from his position? Joseph was holy when the temptation came. He did not try to get holy at that moment. He lived with the burdens being removed and the yokes continually being destroyed. Therefore, when the battle came, there was no question that Joseph would be on the Lord's side.

When you are living close to God and are suddenly faced with the most grievous temptation that has ever come before you, the first thing that will come to your mind is how wonderful your intimate relationship with God is, how much breaking covenant with Him would hurt, and how much you would lose if anything happened to that relationship. Then it becomes easy for you to say, as did Joseph, *"How then can I do this great wickedness, and sin against God?"* It was the anointing of holiness in the life of Joseph that prevented him from sinning against God; and it will work for you too.

The holy and sacred relationship that exists between a believer and God is the most valuable of commodities and must never be handled lightly. Holiness protects you from marring that relationship.

Once you have truly taken hold of your call and begun to walk in the burden-removing, yoke-destroying power of God, holiness is not a difficult thing. It comes naturally.

As you walk in the fullness of the anointing of God on your life, you will find yourself automatically wanting to manifest His holiness along with His power, authority and favor. You can live holy because you are *Empowered for the Call.*

# FOURTEEN

# THE DEVELOPMENT OF VIRTUE

*Whereby are given unto us exceeding great and precious promises: that by these ye might be PARTAKERS OF THE DIVINE NATURE, having escaped the corruption that is in the world through lust.* **2 Peter 1:4**

When you tap into the anointing, you are tapping into the virtue of God. What is virtue? It is character. It is the divine nature of God, the essence of His personality and identity. It is what makes God Who He is. Once you have appropriated His holiness, the virtue that develops in your character will follow. Character returns good for evil. Paul wrote:

*Dearly beloved, avenge not yourselves, but rather give place unto wrath: for it is written, Vengeance is mine; I will repay, saith the Lord.*
*Romans 12:19*

When you refuse to get petty, to get into the mud and fight with people — even if they have done you wrong, stolen from you or tried to destroy your good name — God will give it all back to you, and much more. If men violate your rights, it is God's prerogative to take care of it — in His way. If He does not choose to do it the way you wanted to see it done, it is still His business. Character leaves judgment with God.

The dynamic of virtue, which is an integral part of your anointing from God, is one that should be in a continuous process of development in your life as you move toward fulfilling His calling.

### VIRTUE BEGINS WITH OBEDIENCE

Virtue begins with simple obedience. The perfection and virtue of Jesus was not in His miracles. It was in His obedience. The reason He was able to sit down at the right hand of the Father was not because of raising Lazarus or healing the sick. It was because He had obediently suffered all things. He was *"tempted in all points"* even as you are, yet He *"was without sin"* because He obeyed the Father.

He would have liked to see the cup pass from Him, but He set His face toward Jerusalem in obedience, saying, *"Not My will, but Thine be done."* Jesus was not just another man. He was the Anointed One.

Paul wrote to the Romans:

*For if ye live after the flesh, ye shall die: but if ye*

# The Development of Virtue

*through the Spirit do mortify the deeds of the body,*
*ye shall live.*                                    Romans 8:13

Your deposit of the anointing is intended to cause you to develop virtue, so that you will walk uprightly before God, so that *your good will not be evil spoken of.* Your anointing kills your flesh, helps your infirmities, brings revelation, causes you to be edified, and keeps you in freedom. If God can develop His virtue, His character, in you He can truly begin operating through you in an effective level for others.

Never for a moment make the mistake of thinking that operating in holiness and virtue will make you weak. On the contrary! When you devote yourself to the integrity of God, it will cause every muscle of your spiritual anatomy to become bulk, mighty and empowered to do the things of the Spirit.

When the anointing develops virtue in you, there will be a tangible difference. Lying stops, sinful anger stops, stealing stops, corrupt communication stops. Instead of grieving the Holy Spirit and breaking God's heart with your carnal attitudes, you begin doing good things, speaking good things, and producing good fruit.

As you develop a Godlike character, *malice, bitterness* and *anger* will be gone; and in their place will be *"love, joy, peace, longsuffering, gentleness, goodness, faith, meekness, and temperance"* (Galatians 5:22).

## INTEGRITY IN ALL CIRCUMSTANCES

Because holiness was a part of Joseph's life, he was able to maintain his integrity in every circumstance. If he had yielded to the desires of Potiphar's wife, it would have destroyed him. He would have lost his integrity, his purpose in life, and his gift and authority. Anointed people don't take ungodly advantage of a situation. They don't cheat, lie or deceive, but operate in godly virtue instead. It is high time for the church to begin to show some true character.

In this present world it can be difficult and even dangerous to take a stand for what is right instead of what is popular. We must understand the price we will pay socially. But when the anointing of virtue is on our lives, we cannot help ourselves. We simply cannot remain silent.

Anyone can follow the crowd, but those who choose to walk the *"straight and narrow"* way of the Lord will be set apart very quickly.

## YOU CANNOT BE VIRTUOUS IN THE FLESH

You cannot be virtuous in the flesh. Your flesh wants what your flesh wants — *"the lust of the flesh, and the lust of the eyes, and the pride of life"* (1 John 2:16). But when you have the burden-removing, yoke-destroying power of God in operation in your life, it will enable you to live a virtuous life. You will no longer have to struggle with getting too close to the line or too near the things of the flesh. When God's Spirit is allowed to dominate your life, you will *"hunger and thirst after righteousness."*

If you are not committed to living a life of virtue, character and integrity, you can miss out on the fulfillment of the call of God on your life.

Remember, holiness directly impacts your relationship with God, and virtue has an equally significant impact on your relationship with the people around you. How we treat others will impact the flourishing of the power of God in our lives and could potentially slow down the process of our apprehending our destiny.

As you get to truly know the God who called and empowered you, and begin to be more like Him, you will develop His virtuous character and see your anointing of destiny fulfilled. His promise is:

> *And such as do wickedly against the covenant shall he corrupt by flatteries: but the people that do know their God shall be strong, and do exploits.*
> Daniel 11:32

You can be virtuous because you are *Empowered for the Call.*

# PART IV:

# PERFECTING, PROTECTING AND MAINTAINING THE ANOINTING

# PERFECTING THE ANOINTING

*And he gave some, apostles; and some, prophets; and some, evangelists; and some, pastors and teachers; FOR THE PERFECTING OF THE SAINTS, for the work of the ministry, for the edifying of the body of Christ: Till we all come in the unity of the faith, and of the knowledge of the Son of God, unto a perfect man, unto the measure of the stature of the fulness of Christ: That we henceforth be no more children, tossed to and fro, and carried about with every wind of doctrine, by the sleight of men, and cunning craftiness, whereby they lie in wait to deceive;* Ephesians 4:11-14

While it is essential for each of us, as believers, to acknowledge the personal empowerment God has put upon our lives and to understand how it affects the world around us, I would be remiss in a study on the anointing power of God if I did not touch on how this anointing manifests itself specifically in the working of the fivefold ministry.

We have already seen that the gifts and callings of God are without repentance and that when God calls He empowers for that call. The church today has too many examples of well-meaning people who have stepped into one area of the fivefold ministry or another without actually being called of God. Since we know that it is only the God-given anointing power which will remove burdens and destroy yokes, it follows that those who call themselves or allow themselves to be placed by other men into positions of authority in the church structure are defeated before they even begin. Without the burden-removing, yoke-destroying power of God on our lives, no person — no matter how good, well-meaning, or civic-minded — can step behind a pulpit or onto a platform and effectively do the work of an evangelist, apostle, prophet, pastor or teacher.

## BECOMING CHRIST-LIKE IS THE GOAL

The Word of God makes very clear the reasons for the establishment of the fivefold ministry: to build up the Body of Christ, to unify the Body of Christ, to encourage the Body of Christ to have a deeper relationship with God and to perfect the members of the Body of Christ to the point that they actually become Christ-like. The word perfection means "to mature, equip and complete." For the Body of Christ to effectively minister to the needs of society, the anointing of perfection must touch their lives. The accomplishment of any of these goals requires transformation, and without a life-changing anointing being administered, these necessary changes can never take place.

The perfecting anointing that is released through the five unique offices of ministry releases God's people into the work of ministry. Each office has a unique impartation that, when combined with the other ministries and received by the Body of Christ, results in the maturing, equipping and completing of the saints. There must be a mixing together of the anointing of the apostle, prophet, evangelist, pastor and teacher, and when this mix of anointings is received into our spirits, it will cause us to arise into a new level of empowerment.

The anointing represented by the fivefold ministry given by God for the maturing of the saints corresponds to the anointing given by God to the kings of the Old Testament.

## THE KINGLY ANOINTING

*Then Samuel took a vial of oil, and poured it upon his head, and kissed him, and said, Is it not because the LORD hath anointed thee to be captain over his inheritance?* 1 Samuel 10:1

Saul became the first king over the people of Israel and was not anointed to be a prophet or a priest, but to be *"captain over [God's] inheritance."* It was the anointing upon his life that prepared him to rule, and it became his responsibility to watch over the nation of Israel and keep it from sin. To operate under a kingly anointing, true captains over the flock of God must be concerned for the future of their little ones. It is time to teach people how to move in the anointing of God, to move in the creative realms of the Spirit. The kingly anointing releases divine authority that produces the maturing, equipping and completing of those who are the inheritance of the Lord.

Satan is always trying to *"steal, kill and destroy,"* and we need men and women of God who will accept the responsibility of the kingly anointing and become concerned about preserving their faith for the coming generations. God is searching for those He can raise up to protect the future of the Body of Christ in the Earth.

Not all anointed men and women are called to one of the fivefold ministry offices. There are many administrations of the gifts. God can use you in your family, your occupation, your community or your church in any number of ways. There is no particular importance to which calling He has given you. The only importance is in your obedience to that call.

If you are one of those whom God has called to

be a member of the fivefold ministry, it's time to pull up your spiritual bootstraps and step into the anointing of destination God has for you. Remember that when God calls, He empowers. When you are carrying Baby "Calling," you can rest assured that his twin, Baby "Gifting," is snuggled right up there next to him and will be delivered at the same time.

The Word of God assures us that our gifts will make room for us. Don't despair if you have a revelation from God that you are to be used in one of the fivefold ministry gifts, yet it looks as though there is no way your circumstances, background or education will ever allow that to happen. God is not limited by your circumstances, background or education. He cannot be limited by anything.

Your part is to work at developing your *enchrio*. Seek for a closer relationship with the Lord. Get to know Him and His Word. If you can put away fear and doubt, and just trust Him, He will do the rest.

## SUBMITTING TO THE MATURING ANOINTING

Although God has placed the fivefold ministry over the flock to mature it, the responsibility of submitting to that maturing process rests with the individual. Paul taught the Galatians:

*Now I say, That the heir, as long as he is a child, differeth nothing from a servant, though he be lord of all; But is under tutors and governors until the time appointed of the father.*     Galatians 4:1-2

God is looking for those to whom He can entrust the future of the Church and, therefore, it is time for every believer to begin to submit to the maturing anointing, so that we can each make some real progress toward reaching our goal: *"the measure of the stature of the fullness of Christ."* We have had enough scandals, enough men and women failing for lack of character. It is time for serious submission so that God can do the work He desires in each of us.

As long as we remain spiritually childish, we can never possess our prophetic heritage. We must take the time to sit under the instruction of anointed teachers so that we can grow and mature in God and quickly rise to the challenge at hand.

Many people seem to be floundering in the knowledge of their calling. Part of the reason is that they have never completely understood their divine destiny. They have refused to cover themselves with God-given *"tutors and governors"* who could help them understand it more fully. These people resist, refuse to listen and to take instruction. The great danger is that if they stop growing and developing in the very early stages of their spiritual life and will, therefore, not have strength to withstand the onslaught of an enemy who is determined to steal their potential.

## Perfecting the Anointing

When you sit in a service under an anointed ministry, you can either throw up philosophical and psychological walls and refuse to receive what God is saying, or you can open your spirit to the anointed message and reap the benefits. If you allow the anointing to do its work, you will leave every service with a burden removed and with your spirit one rung higher up the ladder of maturity.

Pastors and other Christian leaders must play a significant role in helping others mature in their anointing by setting an example (by flowing in the anointing themselves), and by setting guidelines and establishing parameters for everyone to follow. But even Christian leaders have their limitations. It is impossible for any individual to grow into maturity unless that person is willing to deepen his or her own relationship with the Righteous One, so that *His* righteousness can begin to be manifested in his or her life.

Many have their growth stunted because, when they come to a point where there is a price to pay to walk in the fullness of the empowerment of the anointing of God, they are either totally unwilling or not quite ready yet to pay that price. Since it is neither popular, fashionable, intellectually acceptable, nor politically correct to have God's touch on your life these days, many won't allow God to have His way with them. They actually resist His anointing, considering the price of being misunderstood, despised and accused of pride and self-exaltation too high for them to pay. Therefore they cannot possibly grow into all that God wants them to be and do.

## REVELATION LIFTS THE IMMATURITY

Those who get a true revelation of what God wants for their lives usually see their immaturity lift. Suddenly, they want to be all that God wants them to be more than they want anything else. They will gladly prove themselves, through diligence, holiness and a sincere desire to please God. These people become obvious choices to be entrusted with a portion of God's great inheritance.

As we mature, we stop saying, "Look what I gave up to serve God," and, instead, start saying, "Thank God that I have been delivered from the kingdom of darkness. I gave up nothing and gained everything in exchange." At that point we can know that we have our priorities straight.

Getting to that point, however, can be difficult because of the age-old battle between the flesh and the spirit. But the Bible teaches that the spirit can *"mortify the deeds of the body [flesh]"* and that God can *"bring into captivity every thought to the obedience of Christ."*

As you mature in the anointing, you begin to realize that it is the things for which you have had a genuine affection in life that will most powerfully war against your call in God. There will be some very tough decisions for you to make, and you may be called on to sacrifice family, financial security, and stable employment to do the will of God.

It is worth the risk, however. If you are an *"heir,"* it means that God has something earmarked for your future. It is very much like a promissory note that you can collect down the road. While you are growing, you may operate, now and then, in spurts of your future anointing, but you will come to a place where you can no longer afford the luxury of only operating in the anointing once in a while and will want to jump in with both feet.

## SETTING FORTH TO SPREAD THE GOSPEL

Once God has prepared, equipped and matured you, He can trust you with your anointing of destination and can set you forth to spread the Gospel of the Kingdom, the Gospel of the Anointed One. He is only waiting for your increased maturity to do many of the wonderful things He has shown you over the years.

God wants all the members of the Body of Christ to come into *"the unity of the faith,"* and *"the knowledge of the Son of God."* His will is for you to develop *"unto a perfect man,"* complete and mature in *"the measure of the stature of the fullness of Christ,"* the

Anointed One and His Anointing (power and giftings). What a powerful standard of measurement! The progress that you and I make toward maturity is measured by nothing less than the example of Christ Himself. Strive on toward that exalted goal.

Fulfilling your call, even if it is to be a end-time spiritual leader, does not depend on you. It depends on God, and He is more than able. Submit to Him and to His servants, and your life will be quickly matured, equipped and completed. If you will open your spirit to the kingly perfecting authority, God will do the work. You need not fear for your future, for you are *Empowered for the Call*.

# PROTECTING THE ANOINTING

*Be sober, be vigilant; because your adversary the devil, as a roaring lion, walketh about, seeking whom he may devour: Whom resist stedfast in the faith, knowing that the same afflictions are accomplished in your brethren that are in the world.*

1 Peter 5:8-9

We are living in a world controlled and manipulated by the powers of Hell. When the revelation of the call of God on your life in conceived within you, you become a prime target for the Prince of Darkness. Satan is after your call because he knows that when you are anointed, you have power, authority, favor, holiness and virtue from God, everything you need to bring him to defeat.

The enemy doesn't want you to believe that God dwells in you because he never wants you to get a revelation that you are anointed and that no matter what Hell throws at you, you are free and *"free indeed."* Because of Satan's desire to devour *"whom he may,"* the Word of God shows us that we must be *"sober"* and *"vigilant."* Satan is intent on devouring God's lethal weapons, God's prophets in the making. Satan is an abortionist, wanting to destroy the new life that is being formed within you.

The abortion crisis we are facing in America today, in the natural realm, is nothing more than a direct reflection of the abortion crisis we have in the spiritual realm. The minute you conceive life inside your spiritual womb that old spiritual abortionist will come around, saying, "I'm going to cut the life out of him [or her]. I cannot permit that life to be formed. Those twin babies of "Call" and "Gifting" cannot be allowed to come to birth." You must stop him in his tracks.

## CHOOSE TO USE YOUR GOD-MEMORY

One area the enemy is sure to attack, in an effort to abort your call, is your mind. You were born with a natural, carnal mind that is constantly at war with God and is *"not subject to the law of God."* So Satan endeavors to keep at the forefront of your carnal mind, not what God is saying to you, but criticism, rejection and hateful accusations. Your anointing, however, has a God-memory. The Holy Ghost, the Scriptures promise, *"brings to ... remembrance"* everything the Lord has spoken and will help your mind to overcome Satan's onslaught.

## Protecting the Anointing

Satan will tell you that you're going to fail, but the Holy Ghost will bring back to your remembrance every promise the Lord has given you. The enemy will fill your carnal mind with fear, telling you that you're going to get sick or die with a dreaded disease like cancer. He will even remind you of family members who died at an early age. The Holy Ghost will bring back to your remembrance the things the Lord says in this regard. It may be through the Scriptures, it may be through personal prophecy, or it may be in some other way. But whether from the Psalms or one of the Gospels, or a dream or a vision or a prophecy, your anointing will always remind you of the report of the Lord, and will show the enemy up for what he is — a liar.

Sometimes it seems easier for us to believe some looming circumstances than it is to believe the simple promises of God. In those moments we must decide whom we will believe. Will we believe the report of the enemy? Or will we rather say, "God has a plan for me. God has a call for my life, so I refuse to give in to these circumstances."

### Satan Doesn't Want Your Stuff
### He Wants You Paralyzed in the Pew

Many believers notice that Satan is targeting their lives in the financial realm and imagine that he wants their money. Although Satan attacks heavily in the area of finances, he's not after your money. He's not after your car or your house or your position. He is targeting the revelation you have of the call of God that is on your life. Satan knows that it is the knowledge of the divine destiny of God in your life which makes you a lethal weapon against him.

Satan wants to burden you down under the circumstances of life. When you have problems, you will think about those problems most of the time. If there is trouble in your marriage, if your child becomes rebellious and begins to experiment with alcohol, drugs or sexual promiscuity, or if you are physically sick and in constant pain, your mind will most likely become focused on those circumstances. As a result, you will not focus on God and His call on your life.

If you allow yourself to get in a spiritually weakened condition, feeling discouraged and depressed, the devil will try to get his yoke around your neck. But don't yield to his wishes. Let some of that *enchrio* anointing go down into your spirit, so that you can begin to look at things differently. When Satan tries to put his yoke around your neck, instead of being weak and feeble and succumbing to his evil purpose, let that anointing remind you of the revelation of who you are in God. Recognize that you are so big in God that Satan's yoke just will not fit on you.

Satan's attitude is that if you are saved and go to

Heaven, so be it. But he wants to prevent you from accepting your call. If he can rob you of your call, you will become paralyzed in the pew. You may go to Heaven, but at least you won't be taking anybody with you: When you are burdened down, you won't be praying for the sick and seeing them recover. You won't be a mighty spiritual warrior, interceding for the Body of Christ. The real reason Satan fights you — financially, relationally and physically — is not because he's interested in your money, marriage or health. He's a thief who has come *"to steal, kill and destroy,"* and he's trying to bury your call and the revelation of that call by bombarding you with problems.

Another reason Satan goes after your loved ones and your most prized possessions is because he is determined to put a spirit of discouragement on you so that you will give up on the life of God growing inside of you. He wants you to bury your gift and call.

## HOW TO DEFEAT DISCOURAGEMENT

When Satan targets you for discouragement, what can you do? You can learn from David. When David and his men had virtually lost everything at Ziklag, the enemy came at him in a flood of discouragement, but the Word of God tells us:

> *And David was greatly distressed; for the people*
> *spake of stoning him, because the soul of all the*
> *people was grieved, every man for his sons and*
> *for his daughters: but David encouraged himself*
> *in the* LORD *his God.*          1 Samuel 30:6

*"David encouraged himself in the Lord."* I believe he did this by speaking over and over to himself the things that God had spoken to him, reminding himself that he was called to be king.

Paul wrote to his spiritual son Timothy:

> *This charge I commit unto thee, son Timothy, ac-*
> *cording to the prophecies which went before on*
> *thee, that thou by them mightest war a good war-*
> *fare.*          1 Timothy 1:18

God has given us the prophecies concerning our call and destiny, not just to make us feel good, but to give us a weapon with which we can war against the spirit of discouragement. When David did this, he became bold in his spirit again and began to pray and to hear from God. As a result, he went after his adversary and took back everything that had been stolen from him.

In the midst of this whole trial, David's men turned on him and even wanted to stone him. When you begin to move in the manifestation of the gifts of the Spirit, you can count on all Hell breaking loose around you. Satan will make sure that demons and carnal men do everything in their power to bury your gift and call.

Deciding to allow God's anointing to rest upon you and work through you will not result in the formation of a fan club. Don't expect everyone to like you. Don't expect everyone to praise you. You can expect criticism. You can expect to be misunderstood. You can expect people to get in your face. You can even expect some people to hate you, branding you as "dangerous," "radical" or "extremist."

Your enemy will never tire of reminding you of what people think about you or say about you. If he can bury your anointing in gossip or rejection, he will do it. Many people just can't handle such rejection. They are fine as long as everyone around them agrees with them, but when anyone takes exception to what they are saying or doing, they allow it to distract them from their appointed purpose. You must come to a place in your life where you reject rejection and cling to the promise of God.

## RECOGNIZE THE LIE

When someone speaks something that is a direct contradiction to the plan of God for your life, you must recognize it for the lie that it is and reject it immediately. Don't even entertain the thought or let it become part of your thinking. Give the enemy a black eye by getting free from all the lies that have become a part of your thinking. Let God do this for you.

When God exalted Joseph, it made no difference what his brothers had thought or said about him. It made no difference what Potiphar's wife had accused him of. It made no difference what any of his fellow prisoners or any of the prison officials in the jail had thought or said about him. When the king gave Joseph full authority, nothing else mattered. As an anointed vessel for God, you have been given the authority of the King of kings, and nothing else should matter.

The Word of God promises:

> *No weapon that is formed against thee shall prosper; and every tongue that shall rise against thee in judgment thou shalt condemn. This is the heritage of the servants of the* Lord, *and their righteousness is of me, saith the* Lord.
>
> Isaiah 54:17

No lie can defeat you, and no deception can prevent you from doing God's will. Know that you are an anointed man or woman of God and destined for greatness. The Lord has guaranteed your victory because you walk in His anointing.

Yes, there will be battles. Yes, the enemy is angry and will use all the powers of Hell to attempt to destroy you. You may well become a walking target for Satan and his legions of demons, but never mind the fact that he is fighting you every step of the way. All his tricks put together cannot defeat the anointing of God that is on your life.

## PUTTING THE ANOINTING FIRST

There must come a time when we each place our call from God as our number-one priority, a time when we no longer care what the cost is, and when we are willing to walk away from anything of the flesh that once held our affections. We must become willing to say, "Lord, doing what You have called me to do is more important to me than anything else in this world."

Satan will not be pleased with this decision, and he will try, with every weapon in his arsenal, to pull you back toward the things of the flesh and to entice you to lower your guard. Fight back with every fiber of your being to protect the gifts, the callings and the empowerment of your anointing. A sure test of spiritual maturity is a willingness to protect the anointing at all costs, to refuse to allow anything to take a position in your life that could hinder or dilute it in any way. Let nothing hold back or jeopardize the fulfillment of your call.

There *is* an empowerment that comes with the call, but there is also a price to be paid that you might know, understand and fully receive all that God has promised. You must bring your vessel under subjection to God to the point that you are ready to say, as Jesus did, *"Not my will, but Thine be done."*

When you do this, you need fear nothing. You have the victory, for you are *Empowered for the Call.*

# MAINTAINING THE ANOINTING

*How God anointed Jesus of Nazareth with the Holy Ghost and with power: who went about doing good, and healing all that were oppressed of the devil; for God was with him.*     Acts 10:38

The anointing is not just for Sunday services. It is not just for reaching out in ministry to the sick, the hurt and the lost. It must be an integral part of every area of our lives, and we must learn to maintain it so that it is there when we most need it.

Jesus was anointed by God and the result was that He *"went about doing good."* Good is a product of the anointing and should become such a part of our lives that *"all thing work together for good"*:

*And we know that all things work together for good to them that love God, to them who are the called according to his purpose.*     Romans 8:28

There may be times when we don't feel that everything is working for good in our lives, but what the Lord is trying to impress on us is that the anointing is working in every aspect of our lives to make it a finely tuned machine. Every part of that machine must work together to produce good results.

When we are together in a church service there is a certain level of agreement of purpose and faith; but when we are out in the trenches, face to face with the atheist, the agnostic, the immoral, the uncaring and the uncompassionate, that's when we really need the empowerment of God to be manifest. God would be unfaithful if He anointed us to teach a Sunday School class and then left us on our own when we were working in a factory. It is when we face the world that we need every dynamic of our anointing to be manifested — the power, the authority, the favor, the holiness and the virtue.

As an anointed vessel, fit for the Master's service, you must have more to offer than words. You must have *"rivers of living water"* flowing from your innermost being, and not just when you are asked to give the opening prayer in a particular service or share your testimony at a Bible study. You need to have the burden-removing, yoke-destroying power of God coming forth from you — no matter where you are and no matter who you happen to be with at the time.

What God did for Joseph He can do for you, too.

## Maintaining the Anointing

Joseph refused to allow circumstances to affect him, and you must do the same. God is God, and He never changes; so His anointing is always the same, no matter what happens around you. Joseph was anointed in his father's house, he was anointed in the pit, he was anointed in Potiphar's house, he was anointed in the prison, and he was anointed when he came to power. Too many people only feel anointed when everything is going right. That is a major mistake. The anointing is not a feeling. It is the empowerment of God to fulfill His call on your life, and that never changes, regardless of your circumstances. You must not only have it in church; you must maintain it daily so that you go *"from glory to glory."*

### GOING *"FROM GLORY TO GLORY"*

Once God has given you power and authority, you may begin moving in demonstrations of that power. It is when you move into God's favor, however, and begin manifesting His holiness and virtue, that you will truly see that His work in your life is beginning to have a positive influence over those around you. This will have more impact than giving a prophetic word or praying for a sick person. It will carry that burden-removing, yoke-destroying power of God into every area of your life, into every decision you make that will impact your family, community or church.

It is only after you become willing to humble yourself before God and seek His face that the anointing power can move in your life and break the yokes of rejection, anger, bitterness and unforgiveness. Then the transformation of the Anointed One and His Anointing (power and giftings) will become real in your life, and your relationships will become examples of the manifestation of the fruits of the Spirit.

If you want blessed children, one sure way to get them is to let the anointing power of God kill your flesh. When a father and mother walk uprightly before God, choosing not to avenge a wrong, passing by the opportunity to take advantage of someone, choosing words of encouragement rather than despair in difficult times, they become role models who will encourage their children to live godly lives and to desire the anointing power of God on them as well.

## DISPLAYING THE FRUITS

You can recognize a truly anointed person by the fruit evident in his or her relationships. An anointed person doesn't cheat or deal unfairly in business. An anointed person doesn't cause strife among brothers or division or confusion in the Body. An anointed person keeps himself under control, exercises good judgment and helps resolve problems. An anointed person doesn't listen to the reports of the world when they conflict with the Word of God. An anointed person doesn't bend to the pressures of ungodly authority. Like Shadrach, Meshach and Abed-nego, persons who are empowered by God must know with every fiber of their being that even if the fires of adversity are heated up seven times hotter, God will step into the picture and manifest Himself in the midst of their circumstances.

Proverbs shows us:

> *The integrity of the upright shall guide them: but the perverseness of transgressors shall destroy them.*          Proverbs 11:3

Saul made a fatal mistake. He thought that just because he had once been anointed by God he didn't need to maintain his relationship with God or work on relationships with those around him. The eroding of his *enchrio* to the point of rebellion against God eventually caused the *epichrio* to cease operating in his life altogether.

If you allow your *enchrio* to erode, you will soon find that jealousy, gossip and intolerance will destroy your valued relationships. You will become isolated and lose the trust of those around you, and this will cause you to lose opportunities to exercise your *epichrio*.

When you walk in the empowerment of the Anointed One, you will manifest God's love, and it will automatically be reflected in all your relationships. Jesus said:

> *By this shall all men know that ye are my disciples, if ye have love one to another.*   John 13:35

Let the anointing of God permeate all your deeply personal relationships, and you will not be disappointed by the result.

As an anointed man and woman, you must stop relegating your anointing to what you might previously have thought of as "an appropriate occasion." Develop an anointed lifestyle, and let the oil of anointing permeate every part of your being.

One of the most important ways we can maintain the anointing is through developing a consistent life of worship before the Lord. By doing this we are fulfilling the priestly anointing of the Old Testament.

## THE PRIESTLY ANOINTING

> *Ye also, as lively stones, are built up a spiritual house, an holy priesthood, to offer up spiritual sacrifices, acceptable to God by Jesus Christ.*
> 1 Peter 2:5

## Maintaining the Anointing

The priestly anointing prepares us principally to offer spiritual sacrifices, which are *"acceptable to God."* The Old Testament priests kept incense burning continually on the Golden Altar, symbolic of our prayer and praise, and the smoke of that sweet-smelling incense rose up to Heaven twenty-four hours a day, seven days a week.

Prayer is a critical part of spiritual sacrifice. God has a plan for our lives, and Satan will do anything he can to disrupt that plan. If we fail to acquire enough wisdom to tear down the strongholds of the enemy and to build up the hedges against him, we might find ourselves halted between two opinions, stuck in the middle. Just as the Golden Altar burned constantly, we must be men and women who *"pray without ceasing"* and who teach others to do the same. The joy that this brings to your life is crucial to your success as a believer.

When we think of being anointed of God, we tend to think automatically of power, gifts and blessings, and may not consider the relationship of joy and praise to the empowerment of our call. Yet joy (and the praise and worship it produces in us) are a vital and integral part of the anointing power of God. It would be impossible to teach on the anointing without covering the anointing of joy, since it is one of the means God uses to lift burdens and destroy yokes.

Joy, in the case of the believer, must never be a

reaction to circumstances. Happiness may be. We feel happy because we have a new car or a new house. Joy, on the other hand, is a manifestation of God's anointing power in our lives and cannot be produced any other way. Because God is the only source of the anointing, He is the only source of joy. He desires to anoint His people *"with the oil of gladness"*:

*Thou lovest righteousness, and hatest wickedness: therefore God, thy God, hath anointed thee with the oil of gladness above thy fellows. All thy garments smell of myrrh, and aloes, and cassia, out of the ivory palaces, whereby they have made thee glad.*                    Psalms 45:7-8

This prophecy referred directly to Jesus. He was to become the Anointed One and was to be *"anointed above all [His] fellows."* His garments would be drenched with the scents of Heaven, and he would be made *"glad."* Since we are the successors of Jesus' ministry, however, and since He had *"the oil of gladness"* poured upon Him, we have the right to have that same oil applied to our lives. We are to be anointed as He was anointed. The anointing of joy and gladness is part of our God-given birthright as an anointed servant of God. Why should we receive part of that birthright and deny the rest?

Jesus found joy in His mission in life. He found

joy in ministering to those around Him. His joy in no way depended on His circumstances. It was a consequence of His relationship to God.

While we may sometimes be moved by a powerful anointing of joy in a service and find ourselves lying on the floor laughing, joy is much more than that. It is recognizing that the Lord is worthy of praise — wherever we happen to be and whatever the circumstances we happen to face at the moment. This type of joy is so exciting and contagious that it will affect everyone around us.

## HE IS PRESENT IN OUR PRAISE

We desperately need the literal, tangible presence of God to be manifested in our churches today. We all recognize the need to have His power working freely in our midst. But how are to bring that about? The answer is very simple. The Word of God teaches us that the Lord *"inhabits the praises of His people."* Therefore, when anointed praise is going forth, He is present, and as His presence permeates the atmosphere, joy will build.

David exalted:

> *Thou wilt show me the path of life: in thy presence is fulness of joy; at thy right hand there are pleasures for evermore.* Psalms 16:11

If it all seems so simple and direct, but why then are both the power and joy of the anointing of the Lord so often absent in our churches and in our personal lives? It is because Satan also understands the power of anointed praise and joy. He was the anointed cherub before his fall, so he is Heaven's ex-choir director. As such, he recognizes that he must do everything he can to suppress our praise and steal our joy.

Satan will do all he can to keep the people of God from practicing a biblical pattern of praise — clapping, singing, shouting and dancing with joy before the Lord — and, because he knows how to appeal to our flesh, how to appeal to the pride in our carnal natures, he tries to get us to think we are "too spiritual," "too deep" to praise God in a "fanatical" way.

## The Deeper You Go, the More Freely You Praise

Don't ever let the enemy deceive you into thinking that you are "too deep to praise God." That is religious intellectualism. If you lose the simplicity of joyful, biblical praise, you have lost it all. The truth of the matter is that the deeper you go in God, the more freely and joyfully you will want to praise Him. Praising God with reckless abandonment is one way of expressing the realization of the value He and His anointing have in your life. After all, praise is the very reason we were created. Isaiah declared:

*This people have I formed for myself; they shall show forth my praise.*               Isaiah 43:21

If you have let Satan deceive you and rob you of the joy of praise, it's not too late. If you have allowed the circumstances of your life to get you down, there is something you can do. If you are void of joy, let God restore your spirit. Your circumstances may not change, but your method of dealing with them will. You can again experience the joy of God's presence. Exercise you priestly anointing and begin by offering *"a sacrifice of praise."* By offering praise, even in the midst of distressing circumstances, you become a participant in your our own miracle.

As you choose to let the power of the anointing God has placed in your life work to remove the burden of your circumstance and break the yokes of depression and despair, you will free yourself to worship in freedom and joy. You will rejoice in the same anointing of joy and gladness that Jesus displayed. This is your birthright as the anointed of the Lord, and by exercising it, you can maintain God's anointing upon your life and ministry.

You can do it, for you are *Empowered for the Call.*

# THE CONCLUSION

*And the spirit of the LORD will come upon thee,
and thou shalt prophesy with them, and shalt be
turned into another man. And let it be, when these
signs are come unto thee, that thou do as occasion
serve thee; for God is with thee.*

1 Samuel 10:6-7

If I had to choose one phrase from Scripture which
best expresses the empowerment of the anointing
of God on our lives, it would be this declaration of
the prophet Samuel when he anointed Saul: *"and
thou shalt he turned into another man."* That's what
the anointing power is all about. The law of the
anointing exemplified in the life of Jesus, the
Anointed One, is that where the anointing power of
God is present burdens will be removed and yokes
will be destroyed.

That sounds nice, but how do we accomplish it?
In order for us, as believers, to be empowered for
the call, it is necessary for each of us to be turned
into *"another man."* Our flesh will never accomplish
anything of value to the Kingdom of God. Our carnal minds cannot grasp the keys to operating in
God's power. To truly receive the revelation of the

anointing into our spirits, a revelation which will enable us to endure the period of preparation and then step into our God-ordained destination, we must be willing to pay whatever price is necessary. We must be willing to die to the old man and be turned into *"another."*

Once that transformation — that renewal of our minds — has taken place, God can begin to manifest the burden-removing, yoke-destroying power in our lives. We will have the *enchrio*, the anointing in us for our own personal edification, working within us to begin to mold us into the image of Christ. Then we can begin to operate in the *epichrio*, the anointing which comes upon us and enables us to be a blessing to others.

As more believers begin to walk in this empowerment, the supernatural will become normal for us. We will see people being saved, healed, delivered and set free — as happened with the first-century believers. It is sure to happen when we have truly turned into *"another man"* and when we set forth, empowered for the call, walking in the power, authority, favor, holiness and virtue of the Anointed One.

I trust God, and He promised me that if I was obedient to put forth this message, He would cause it to change lives, would cause men and women to experience a breakthrough in their spirits that would lead them to become rooted, grounded and established. Now that I have done my part, I know He will be faithful to fulfill His promise.

When all true believers, regardless of denominational affiliation, culture, race, age or education, grasp the importance of allowing God to turn them *"into another man"* for His glory, and when more of us have set forth to fulfill His call in our lives, we will begin the transformation necessary to form us into the glorious Bride our Savior anxiously awaits. Be *Empowered for the Call.*

*And the spirit of the LORD will come upon thee, and thou shalt prophesy with them, and shalt be turned into ANOTHER MAN.*

1 Samuel 10:6

# *Other Books*

## POSSESSING YOUR PROPHETIC PROMISE

At a time when the church has been blessed by the greatest period of expository teaching of the Word of God than any generation has experienced, at a time when we have more resources available to us then ever before, why do so many of God's people seem to wander for years in the wilderness without ever experiencing a breakthrough into the fullness of what God has promised to them? Why have so many received miraculous provision and protection but still have not scratched the surface of their spiritual potential? It is time to possess our prophetic promises.

But what must we do to cross over the river Jordan and possess our Promised Land? What steps are necessary to dislodge every enemy and take back what is rightfully ours?

As only he can, Dr. Tim Bagwell brings forth the revelation that God has given him to bring YOU to the place of *Possessing Your Prophetic Promise.*

Perfect bound. 168 pages. ISBN 1-885369-12-X     $9.99

# *by Dr. Tim Bagwell*

## WHEN I SEE THE BLOOD

- *Why is it that modern-day Christians have chosen to virtually ignore the message of the blood of Christ?*

- *Why is it that this all-important theme is not being preached more, sung more, and taught more these days?*

- *Could it be that the enemy of our souls is trying to silence a message that is most important to the welfare of our souls and our continuing victory as Christians?*

With convincing authority, Tim Bagwell, declares that the age-old message of the cross is still valid for our time and that many of the false doctrines that have invaded the church today have come about because we have left the truths of Calvary.

*"When Jesus spilled His blood, all Heaven rejoiced to see that the ransom had been paid. There is now absolutely nothing that Satan can do about it. His hold on us has been broken forever."*

Perfect bound. 182 pages. ISBN 1-885369-74-X     $9.99

*Notes*

*Notes*

*Notes*

*Notes*

*Notes*

# ABOUT THE AUTHOR

**DR. TIM BAGWELL** has been acclaimed as a twentieth century prophet and as one of the greatest preachers to ever grace the American platform. He has touched hundreds of thousands of lives since the early 1970s.

His ministry, through evangelistic crusades, conferences and seminars, has taken him across the U.S. and to many other nations of the world, preaching the uncompromised Word of God with signs following. He has ministered in Canada, Haiti, Norway, Holland, Switzerland, the Middle East and Brazil.

Pastors throughout the world solicit his ministry because of its balance of pastoral and evangelistic experience. The churches he ministers in are blessed by the gifts of the Spirit and the bold, uncompromising ministry of the Word.

His book *"Possessing Your Prophetic Promise"* was released in 1995. He and his wife Gayla also released a music album, *Living the Legacy* that same year. In 1996, the first edition of this book was released and in 1998 both this updated version and a new book, *When I See the Blood*, appeared.

The Bagwells have been married since 1975 and have two sons: Adam and Aaron.

Dr. Bagwell currently serves as senior pastor of The Word of Life Christian Center in the metropolitan Denver, Colorado, area.

Ministry address:

**Dr. Tim Bagwell**
**7498 S. Clarkson**
**Littleton, CO  80122**